Paul Mattick: Selected Texts

Historical Materialism Book Series

The Historical Materialism Book Series is a major publishing initiative of the radical left. The capitalist crisis of the twenty-first century has been met by a resurgence of interest in critical Marxist theory. At the same time, the publishing institutions committed to Marxism have contracted markedly since the high point of the 1970s. The Historical Materialism Book Series is dedicated to addressing this situation by making available important works of Marxist theory. The aim of the series is to publish important theoretical contributions as the basis for vigorous intellectual debate and exchange on the left.

The peer-reviewed series publishes original monographs, translated texts, and reprints of classics across the bounds of academic disciplinary agendas and across the divisions of the left. The series is particularly concerned to encourage the internationalization of Marxist debate and aims to translate significant studies from beyond the English-speaking world.

For a full list of titles in the Historical Materialism Book Series available in paperback from Haymarket Books, visit: www.haymarketbooks.org/series_collections/1-historical-materialism.

Paul Mattick: Selected Texts

Edited by
Gary Roth

Haymarket Books
Chicago, IL

First published in 2024 by Brill Academic Publishers, The Netherlands
© 2024 Koninklijke Brill NV, Leiden, The Netherlands

Published in paperback in 2025 by
Haymarket Books
P.O. Box 180165
Chicago, IL 60618
773-583-7884
www.haymarketbooks.org

ISBN: 979-8-88890-553-1

Distributed to the trade in the US through Consortium Book Sales and Distribution (www.cbsd.com) and internationally through Ingram Publisher Services International (www.ingramcontent.com).

This book was published with the generous support of Lannan Foundation, Wallace Action Fund, and the Marguerite Casey Foundation.

Special discounts are available for bulk purchases by organizations and institutions. Please call 773-583-7884 or email info@haymarketbooks.org for more information.

Cover art and design by David Mabb. Cover art is a development of *Painting 41, Rhythm 69 (William Morris Block Printed Pattern Book, with a Hans Richter Storyboard, developed from Richter's* Rhythmus 25 *and Kazimir Malevich's film script* Artistic and Scientific Film – Painting and Architectural Concerns – Approaching the New Plastic Architectural System*).* Paint and wallpaper on canvas (2007).

Printed in the United States.

Library of Congress Cataloging-in-Publication data is available.

Contents

Introduction   1
    Gary Roth

1   Obsessions of Berlin   10

2   Authority and Democracy in the United States   26

3   Interview with Paul Mattick (1972)   40

4   Fascism and the Middle Class   46

5   Capitalism and Ecology   51

6   New Essays   70

7   Dynamics of the Mixed Economy   76

8   Henryk Grossman and Crisis Theory   92

9   Value Theory and Capital Accumulation   106

10   Marxism and Its Critics   127

Works Cited   135
Translations and Sources   137
Index   138

Introduction

Gary Roth

If Paul Mattick (1904–1981) is still worth reading, it is because he brought together several strands of radical thought that retain their currency in today's world.[1] He also serves as an excellent guide to the social and economic upheavals of the past century. Besides Karl Marx, the major influences on Mattick were Rosa Luxemburg, Anton Pannekoek, Karl Korsch, and Henryk Grossman. Together, they define the set of ideas and politics that crystallised under the rubric of 'council communism', that is, the belief that the crisis tendencies within capitalism reassert themselves periodically and with devasting effect and that the organisation of directly controlled councils is the best means to abolish existing social hierarchies and prevent the rise of new ones.

This collection opens with essays reflective of contemporary events. The first piece, 'Obsessions of Berlin', chronicles the subjugation of Berlin in the days and months immediately following the Second World War. For Berlin substitute Gaza City (Palestine), Mariupol (Ukraine), Grozny (Chechnya), Aleppo (Syria), Sanaa (Yemen), or Marawi (Philippines) for descriptions of the bombing campaigns, conquests, and occupations that torment recent times. Part journalism, part editorial and analysis, 'Obsessions of Berlin' draws on newspaper and film reports, renewed contact with colleagues following a decade of fascist dictatorship and war that made communication impossible, letters from friends who travelled to Berlin as part of the postwar relief efforts, and Mattick's own brief, month-long visit in 1948.

The most emotional of Mattick's essays, 'Obsessions of Berlin' is also a piece that closes the previous era for him stylistically, reminiscent as it is of essays he wrote during the 1930s when current developments, rather than prevailing trends, were a major focus of his reportage. The piece is unusual because it appeared in a journal (*Partisan Review*, October 1948) not confined to the radical left, seemingly a 'break-through' moment that foretold a wider audience, a moment that nonetheless disappeared quickly.

The radical left tradition of which Mattick was one of its most forceful exponents was only partially consonant with the critical left that developed in the United States during the postwar era. Unique about Mattick's left was its ability to take equal aim at East and West, the Americans as well as the Russians,

---

1 Passages of this essay appeared originally in Roth 2013.

their mutually reinforced and debased motivations, the thoroughly planned yet needless suffering to which entire populations were subjected, their cynical posturing and diplomatic manoeuvring, and the blatant lies that they paraded as truths. Mattick's even-handed treatment proved too much for an American left that increasingly felt compelled to take sides in conflicts between the superpowers.

The second essay in this collection, 'Authority and Democracy in the United States', addresses the ever-pronounced tendency within democratic systems to produce authoritarian regimes. In the essay, Mattick discusses two interrelated themes: on the one hand, why a socialist movement of consequence never took hold in the United States, and on the other, why fascism has been absent as well. For Mattick, economic crises provoke deep-seated and extreme efforts to either correct or else alter the social system. Thus, 'fascism was an attempt to secure the threatened capitalist system by political and organisational means'. In the United States, however, intermediate solutions were possible by means of the 'mixed economy', that is, large-scale government intervention into the private sector.

Several of these themes are echoed in the response to questions that were sent to Mattick by a European correspondent, translated for the first time here as 'Interview with Mattick, 1972'. What seemed evident then seems to hold true for today as well. As far as the United States was concerned, 'a fascist mass mobilisation is still as unlikely as the emergence of a socialist mass movement', since 'both "right-wing" and "left-wing" radicalism remain marginal phenomena that can be controlled with customary police measures'. In the half-century since this was written, the security forces have only grown stronger. But then as now, Mattick's characteristic optimism about the development of a working-class democracy in the form of councils shines through. This is because the current situation, when imagined in terms of deepening crisis tendencies, 'says nothing about the future'.

A look back at fascism during the early decades of the twentieth century is provided by the essay 'Fascism and the Middle Class'. Written in 1939 for a journal published by council communists in New York City, the piece contrasts in surprising ways the political inclinations of the old middle class of independent proprietors and business owners with the new, salaried middle classes. Deteriorating economic situations led in contradictory directions, depending on the relative strengths of the respective bourgeoisies and labour movements. Included in Mattick's discussion is a quick comparison between fascist Germany and bolshevik Soviet Union, both of which – despite their differences – were shaped by bounded economic situations that catered to heightened ideological and material responses.

Another example of Mattick's application of a marxian analysis to contemporary developments is his essay 'Capitalism and Ecology', also translated specially for this volume. It begins oddly because of its initial focus on the second law of thermodynamics, the Club of Rome and its proposals to curb population growth, and the ecological disasters typical of the state-run systems extant during the late 1970s in Eastern Europe and Asia. After the first few paragraphs, however, the essay broadens into the still urgent issues regarding the destruction of the earth as a form of profit-seeking behaviour. One of the essay's great merits is its ability to relate the ecological crisis to the underlying economic problems that beset the global system, issues that cannot be resolved independently of one another.

1 Mattick's Radicalism

Mattick's radicalism dates to the interwar era, during which a thorough-going critique emerged of the two dominant tendencies that represented marxian socialism, that of the Social Democratic Party in Germany and the Bolsheviks in Russia. Mattick came of age politically when the latter was just beginning to eclipse the former in terms of influence within the European political scene. In other words, Mattick experienced first-hand the disintegration of the traditional labour movement during and immediately after the First World War.[2]

Mattick's parents had been unskilled migrants who moved to Berlin from the countryside not long before his birth in 1904. His father toiled as a lower-level construction and transportation employee who eventually secured stable employment at the huge Siemens machinery complex. His mother worked as a day labourer, washing laundry in other people's homes. Mattick and his three sisters largely raised themselves, the normal state of existence for working-class families. His father was also active in the union movement and the Social Democratic Party. By the start of the First World War in 1914, this party counted 120,000 members in Berlin alone and dominated the local and national political scenes. Mattick's apprenticeship at Siemens began four years later and coincided with the breakdown of German society at the end of the war.

Even before this, the Matticks had been drawn to the left wing of the labour movement. From an early age, Mattick's father had enrolled him in a social democratic youth group that tended to be a collection point for radicals and

---

[2] For a biographical account that emphasises Mattick's political development, rather than his theoretical evolution, and draws heavily from his correspondence, see Roth 2015.

anti-militarism advocates. His father was drafted during the war and returned home as part of the anti-war minority within socialist circles. This minority had deep roots in the labour movement and was highly sceptical of the electoral successes and social reforms that the party had emphasised during the previous few decades. This same scepticism, of course, had long been true for the anarchists and syndicalists, but marxism too produced its dissenting groups. In Germany, this opposition coalesced around Luxemburg, among others. In the immediate aftermath of the war, all three currents – anarchism, syndicalism, and radical marxism – amalgamated briefly but powerfully in some of the political groups to which the young Mattick belonged.

The radicals were particularly attuned to the cyclical nature of capitalist development, which they understood in two corresponding ways and which would find further elaboration in Mattick's work. For one, recurring, even if mostly short-lived, recessions and business downturns prompted widespread resistance and anti-capitalist sentiments that swelled the socialist movement. But also, secondarily, these same alternating phases of prosperity and depression explained the splits and fragmentation that had emerged within the labour movement. Increasingly, the various socialist, social democratic, and labour parties as well as the various workplace unions and syndicates throughout the industrialising world came to believe that significant improvements in wages, working and living conditions, and democratic representation were possible because of the rapid unfolding of the capitalist system. A strong and unified social movement, they thought, could reshape capitalism to benefit the working class.

The war shattered these beliefs. Not only had it been destructive on an unprecedented scale, with civilian and military deaths counted in the millions, but with few exceptions, the labour movement had supported the war efforts of their respective countries. Internationalism, so important on an ideological level, had proven to be an empty concept. The Social Democratic Party in Germany, for instance, actively cooperated with the military authorities so that workplace troublemakers were quickly drafted and sent to the front.

Following the First World War, the victorious socialist movements in Germany and Russia used their newly acquired governmental power to suppress the radicals within their own ranks. This was also unprecedented. Until then, internal socialist politicking had been confined to power struggles regarding the use of party finances, appointed positions within the organisations' bureaucracies, and the selection of editors for party-subsidised newspapers. At most, individuals might be expelled from a particular organisation, but the thought of arrests and executions of socialists by other socialists had been unimaginable.

It was in this context of overriding gloom that the radicals re-evaluated workers councils as a locus of revolution and organisation. Everywhere, the councils arose when existing centres of power disintegrated. In Germany, these were primarily workplace councils, some of which served as grievance committees vis-à-vis management and the government, while in other places, they took over managerial functions directly. Soldiers had their own version of councils. In Russia, poor peasants and sharecroppers had theirs too. In both places, citywide councils took on responsibility for municipal and regional affairs. They established committees to run police departments and security agencies, regulated public transportation, arranged food shipments and the distribution of essential consumption items, produced theatre productions and public service announcements, and much more.

Councils were easy to form and had enormous potential. They were flexible and democratic. They presupposed cooperation and coordination, and they extended notions of popular governance and grassroots participation. For council members, neither pre-existing organisations nor a background in socialist theory were prerequisites. Councils made the unions and political parties redundant. They could embrace as much of the population as prevailing political understandings and cultural prejudices made possible. Because of the councils, society was both thrown into chaos and was susceptible to a thorough and radical reorganisation.

The councils could be revolutionary, or they could be nothing much at all – a temporary means to hold society together during a time of crisis and collapse until some facsimile of the old order reconstituted itself. It is for this reason too that Mattick mentions in the 'Interview with Mattick (1972)' that a council system, to be successful, must prevent 'the emergence of a separate state apparatus' that usurps its powers. In both Germany and Russia, the councils ceded their newly won positions of dominance to the socialist organisations that vowed to act on their behalf, the Social Democrats in Germany and the Bolsheviks in Russia, both of whom acted quickly to marginalise the councils.

Mattick had only just begun to work at the Siemens factory complex when the councils arose. Over the next several years, he took part in all the major campaigns initiated by the radical left to either save or extend the council system. These activities, subsequently, formed a point of departure from which he viewed political developments. This would continue to be true after his emigration from Germany and participation in the unemployed movement of the early 1930s in the United States. Here too, Mattick experienced the brief radicalisation of the working class, a moment in which the forms of struggle transcended pre-existing political boundaries. Organisational configurations developed quickly in order to fit immediate situations, and a widespread disregard for the modes of thought that had characterised the working class until that point facilitated the boldness that characterised these many advances.

The piece 'New Essays' provides context for Mattick's political focus during this period. It was written to accompany the republication of the three journals that he helped edit from the mid-1930s until the early 1940s and includes a quick overview of the events and organisations that characterised the revolutionary upheavals that occurred at the end of World War I.

2 Crisis Theory

The First World War ended capitalism's initial period of ascendancy. It had lasted not quite a half-century. The industrial system never stabilised sufficiently such that one could point to a 'classical' era of capitalist development. This in turn deprived observers of a vantage point from which to judge the evolution of society and the economy. For the radical left, Karl Marx's *Capital* served as a substitute because of its ability to unravel basic principles upon which the social system rested. But how to judge the tumultuous developments of the previous few years was far from clear. The pre-war competition among industrial firms seemed to have morphed into a competition between the nations most heavily invested in mechanical production.

As far as the radicals could ascertain, capitalism as a social system had no future, which they referred to as 'the death crisis of capitalism' and which implied an all-out effort to replace it. This, too, put them at odds with Social Democrats and Bolsheviks alike, who each justified their assumption of governmental power through reference to capitalism's renewed tenacity. For Mattick, the death crisis served as the basis from which to view developments of the next decades – repeated recessions and stagnant growth during the 1920s, a deep and seemingly endless depression thereafter, and finally, another horrific world war. Deciphering these profound occurrences became for Mattick themes to which he would return over and over again.

From this perspective, Mattick was one of the few to question the long-term prospects of the brief but powerful post-World War II prosperity. In 'Dynamics of the Mixed Economy', Mattick takes aim at Keynesian solutions to economic problems, that is, governmental attempts to stimulate and stabilise the economy. The essay functions as one of the best, short introductions into this set of issues. The essay also presages Mattick's wider arguments in *Marx and Keynes: The Limits of the Mixed Economy*, a book that remains the deepest exploration yet written about governmental economic activities.

Expressed in language current at the time (state capitalism for a state-run system, waste production for armaments/unproductive expenditures), 'Dynamics of the Mixed Economy' foretells precisely the dilemma in which the global economy remains mired: 'unable to return to the conditions of the past and unable to transform itself into a state capitalist system, the mixed economy alternates between stagnation and destruction, between insufficient capital expansion and increased waste production'. That Mattick emphasised both aspects of this relationship is what distinguished him from liberal and conservative economists alike, who, respectively, either advocated on behalf of government spending or stressed its futility.

This essay and the ones that follow presuppose some familiarity with Marx's theory of capital accumulation as developed in the three volumes of *Capital*. An acquaintance with mainstream economics is also helpful. Mattick's work functions on a high level, with Mattick serving in this regard as somewhat of a theorist's theorist. He was well aware of the limitations with which this saddled him in terms of the accessibility of his work. But no other theory in his opinion provided as much insight into the overriding developmental trends within the capitalist economy, and Mattick took great pains to defend the theory against critics both outside of and within marxism itself.

This is evident in the essay 'Henryk Grossman and Crisis Theory', translated into English for the first time here. It originally appeared as an afterword to a Grossman essay, along with correspondence between Grossman and Mattick from the 1930s. Mattick uses this essay to survey the basic tenets of Marx's theory of capitalist crisis, and thus the essay serves as a good accompaniment to Volume 3 of Marx's *Capital*.

Crisis theory has always been a mainstay of the radical left within marxism. For Mattick, this at first was associated with Luxemburg, and then later with Grossman. Capitalism keeps alive ideas about alternative modes of human existence, if only because it is unable to solve the social and economic problems created in the course of its own development. For Mattick also, capitalism's chronic tendency towards crisis helped contextualise the brutalising attempts to circumvent the market system during the twentieth century, of which fascism in Central Europe and the state capitalism of Russia and elsewhere were salient examples. Mattick defends Grossman against accusations of a mechanistic interpretation of social and economic development, accusations that have a long pedigree, beginning with Marx and aimed at Mattick too.[3]

---

3 For a recent example that refers to Mattick's 'rather mechanical crisis theory' in which 'workers' struggles play no part – except to take advantage of crisis when it occurs', see Cleaver 2017, p. 2n6.

The final two essays, 'Value Theory and Capital Accumulation' and 'Marxism and Its Critics', the latter translated here for the first time, focus on Joseph Gillman. Gillman's attempt to update Marx by revising him is representative of a line of thought that recurs whenever marxism is embraced by new audiences. It is a tradition that first emerged in the years immediately following the deaths of Marx and Engels. Also, the most sophisticated criticisms of marxism have come from within marxism itself, one of the many cultural peculiarities that characterise its history. These criticisms always involve an intense coming-to-terms with primary texts. Thus, Gillman can be considered illustrative of an 'anti-Marx canon' that reappears each time Marx's ideas find widespread resonance and are subjected to renewed scrutiny.

What is this canon? In Gillman's case, it includes an emphasis on the following elements: the overproduction of commodities as the cause for economic slowdowns and collapses – rather than an insufficiency of surplus-value and profit; a focus on the realisation of surplus-value and not on its creation; an emphasis on the rate of profit rather than the mass of surplus-value as the salient factor defining the evolution of the capitalist economy; an attempt to measure values in terms of prices or, alternately, to ignore values altogether and simply discuss the economy in price terms; the relegation of value relationships to a previous era of competitive capitalism rather than the current era; and revolution defined as a post-capitalist society whereby a politically led transformation alters pre-existing economic and social relationships.

That these ideas are often bundled together, as was the case with Gillman, is another of marxism's cultural peculiarities. Both independently and taken as a whole, these revisions transform marxism into an economic science that can thus be measured against other branches of economics in terms of its explanatory and predictive qualities. Marxian economics emerges as a self-anointed conscience of the bourgeoisie, quick to point out the mistaken ideas of an academic field that largely ignores its criticisms anyway.

Because Mattick was not intent on revising Marx, and in fact found his theory of value quite useful, there is a helpful pedagogic quality to Mattick's writings. In other words, Mattick serves as a guide to the understanding of Marx. Mattick emerges as one of the true value theorists within the marxian tradition. There was no need to modernise Marx's explanation of the underlying dynamics that propel the capitalist economy, since these remain constant despite the ever-greater proliferation of commodities which nonetheless thoroughly transform the experiential aspects of social existence. Marx and Mattick interchangeably become the reference points from which to judge the evolution of society and the economy, as well as a means to judge the history of marxism. Whereas the tendency historically has been to short-change Marx intellectually, since he is judged to be either wrong or out-of-date, Mattick uses Marx to reaffirm the central tenets of marxian theory.

Mattick had a complex and unique way of thinking about things. At all points, he focused on the crisis tendencies within capitalism and the implications these held for radical activities. The 'canon' of misconceptions that surround Marx's economic work became a means to test Marx against reality. When Mattick wrote about the working class, it was mostly as a social entity in relationship to capital, not about political subsets within the working class.

During the 1960s and 70s when the economic order unravelled anew, people turned to Mattick for explanations. He was well-known in the new left that was influenced by marxism, mostly in Western Europe: Germany, Italy, and Denmark in particular. Because he was critical of all governmental forms of socialism, and because he did so from a starting point that began within marxism itself, he kept alive a tradition that could be traced back to Luxemburg and others. His unrelenting criticisms of continental socialism and statist regimes alike often meant that state-oriented marxists considered him an anarchist, a label he neither accepted nor rejected.

The issue most important for Mattick was control over the means of production because of the leverage this provides over other aspects of social life. Within marxism, he appealed to its more libertarian currents. The dismantling of the capitalist way of life was for him always synonymous with the abolition of social class distinctions. And although Marx has been prone to a degree of academic normalisation, it is unlikely that this fate will ever befall Mattick.

CHAPTER 1

Obsessions of Berlin

1

As against the terror of the bombs, the actual conquest of Berlin was of lesser significance to its inhabitants. Nevertheless, the artillery tore new holes into the ruins, shot away parts of the surviving buildings, killed many people running for food and water. The spray of machine guns is visible almost on every house, every floor, every apartment door. The tanks ground down the streets and sidewalks. The battle was fought section by section, street by street, house by house. It is said that sixty thousand Russians died in the struggle for Berlin. The estimate may be incorrect, but it reveals the ferocity of the struggle. There are no guesses on the German losses. They lost everything – particularly, however, their illusions about the Russians.

The Russians are Berlin's second great obsession. The rape of the city is burned deep into the minds of its inhabitants because it is associated with their greatest disappointment. Long before the fall of the city, refugees from the East told horrible stories about the Russians' behaviour. So did the radio. But wishful thinking discounted these stories as exaggerations and propaganda. At any rate, it could not get worse than it was. The same hope that welcomed Hitler in exchange for the depression welcomed now the Russians in exchange for the bombings.

Berliners who had once belonged to the Communist Party, or sympathised with it, looked upon the Russian conquerors as their liberators. Their disappointment was consequently greater than that experienced by the great mass of apolitical people and passive Nazis. Even the less exposed Nazis hoped for a quick fall of the city in order to escape a fight that no longer made sense. The more realistic among them killed their families and themselves.

And there were those who had welcomed the Allied bombers in the hope that the misery in their wake would lead to revolt. But the terror-machine of the Nazis proved to be stronger than the despair of the people. The atomisation of the masses was sufficiently advanced to allow the organised terroristic minority to control all situations. But with the Russians at the gates of Berlin, defeatism became more widespread. With the Russians within the city, revolt became possible. But the Russians were not interested; they did not look for help but for loot.

The loot had been promised to the Russian troops – mostly made up of Mongolians – as the price for taking the city. The women were among the spoils.

Despite the disaffection within the German ranks, the fight for Berlin took longer than was expected, the Russian losses were greater than contemplated. The barbarism of the Russian troops is now excused by the ferocity of the Nazi defence that enraged the Russian soldiers. Their rage, it is explained, could not be controlled; it took some time before the Commissars were able to bring order into the chaos and deprive the individual soldier of his right to rape, steal, and kill, in favour of the systematic expropriation executed by the army in the name of the state.

The Nazi stalwarts had the choice of dying fighting or committing suicide. They found it easier to get killed. They hated the Russians and they had no love for the Germans. Whoever was not with them in this last battle was their enemy. Unwilling adolescents and feeble old men were forced into the *Volkssturm*. Those who could not handle a gun, or manipulate a hand-grenade, were kept busy building barricades. Refusal to work or to fight led to immediate execution. Everywhere the defeatists were hanging on the lantern posts. Attempts to cut them down were again punished by death.

The luck of battle shifted from day to day, sometimes from hour to hour. The unwilling soldiers of the *Volkssturm* threw their guns away as soon as the Russians entered their street, only to pick them up again when they were driven back. They would be killed either way: by the Russians if found with a weapon in their hands, by the Nazis if found without their guns. But in the final stages of the battle more and more Germans joined the Russians in the hunting down and killing of the Nazis. They tore down the barricades they had erected to slow the Russian advance. They helped take care of snipers. They recognised the Nazis who had shed their uniforms and destroyed them. They improvised red flags, reorganised the Communist Party, occupied the apartments of Nazi party-members, plundered and killed on their own account.

However, the Russians refused to distinguish between Nazis and anti-Nazis; all Germans were fascists and capitalists. They even outlawed their own German Communist Party, only to allow its legal reorganisation at a much later date – with the arrival of Wilhelm Pieck and his Moscow-picked retinue – so as to have an additional weapon of control. It would not do in May 1945 to offer a Russian soldier a brotherly embrace. He needed just to see the 'luxury' of a radio, watch, or couch to be convinced that he was not dealing with a *Tovarisch* but with a capitalist. At any rate, as he was out to loot, he was not interested in probing the personal history and social position of his victim.

The rape of Berlin was not the aftermath of the struggle but part of it. The fight was less a military affair than a gigantic raid of a million-fold army of bandits. Even the appearance of the Russian soldiers ceased to be military; they discarded filthy and torn parts of their uniforms for German civilian clothes.

They wore two and three suits under the military blouses and pants. Hardly able to walk, they advanced from street to street, tommy-gun in one hand and a suitcase of loot in the other. The bayonet broke open closets and drawers; what was removable was taken, only to be lost again to the Commissars who organised the eastward track of the previously westward Nazi caravans of plunder.

In great demand, of course, were things that could be carried on the body, such as watches and jewellery of all descriptions. As the victory must be celebrated, schnapps and vodka were also in great demand. Every bottle of vinegar was opened and tasted before the Russians accepted their possessors' protestation that they contained no alcohol. And with the schnapps the fighting and thievery gained in élan. Those who could not deliver quickly enough were shot down; women, not willing to give in at once, were thrown out of the windows with their throats slit. Fires were set to the houses that yielded too little, their occupants fleeing the basements into the deadly crossfires of the streets.

During the battle, the interval between life and death is the occasion for love. Stopped for days at a particular spot, there was time for enjoyment before the sniper's bullet found its mark. Women and girls dragged from their basements were lined up on the sidewalks. They tried to make themselves appear old and ugly by smearing their faces with soot and by dirtying the shabby rags they wore in the cellars. But a soldier's hand would wipe away the filth and discover good looks behind the mask of fear. Children would follow their mothers and sisters, only to see them ordered to bend over and lift their skirts to make ready for love in daylight and collectivity, to be loved by drunken soldiers still able, however, to keep an eye on the rooftops so as not to be killed in the act of copulation. Long afterwards, the smaller of the children would play the newly learned 'game of raping'.

The end of the battle is the start of the clean-up period. Groups of Russians began looking for strayed German soldiers; systematically, house by house, block by block. Nights, they returned to be rewarded for their day's troubles. The dead women, sprawling on the streets with their throats cut from ear to ear, served as a terrible reminder not to refuse the victors. The soldiers took what they found, regardless of age. Years without furloughs, years of war and nothing but war, had given them a great and indiscriminate appetite. Lucky the woman who aroused the fancy of an officer who would take charge of her and thus protect her from the mob. For others there was just the command 'stay down ... comrade comes'. It was like in an army brothel; only the experience was missing, and the husband looked on, and the children were not spared. And there was always the fear of death. If the lights suddenly went out, the Russian might start shooting. If the lights suddenly went on, he might also shoot, always suspicious of being trapped, of being tricked, of being surprised by a god-damned German swine.

Of course there are also other stories; stories of the kind Russian soldier who stopped in his fight just to help an old lady cross the street. Stories of the crying Russian soldier killing an old couple to end their useless and hopeless misery. Of the baby-lover, forcing a can of milk down the throat of a terrified child. Of those that took from one German to give to another. Of the Commissar killing the rapist on the spot, and the officer belabouring the plunderer with his sabre. No doubt, these stories are as true as the cruel ones. But the unpredictability of the Russians' behaviour merely increased the fear. Life and death depended on their caprices; it gave the terror a particularly bitter flavour. And when all is said, there remains the fact that within two months Berlin was thoroughly plundered. What was not securely hidden had been taken, most of the women had been mishandled, and the majority of the population had been reduced to paupers.

2

Apparently it was true that the soldiers had lost their discipline. Long after the battle searching parties continued to look in the basements and ruins. They looked no longer for Nazis but for Russians. And they have been looking for deserters ever since; most of the *Razzias* that take place in Berlin have as their first objective the hunt for former Russian soldiers. Troops were shifted, the Mongolians retreated to the hinterland; new soldiers arrived. Too late for the great show they were now forced to buy their women with bread and their bicycles with worthless vouchers and German Marks they had picked up in banks and post offices.

But the troops were still living with the Germans. What kind of people were these Russians? Had they been so totally demoralised by years of campaigning, that they forgot all the so-called civilised ways of behaviour? Or did they come from Russian regions so backward that any comparison with Western standards was at once unfair and impossible? With surprise and contempt the Berliners watched the attempts of Russian soldiers to drill a hole in the wall in the hope that it would spout water just as the faucet did over the kitchen sink. They were amazed by the readiness of the Russian soldier to exchange an expensive wristwatch for any old alarm clock just because it was so much bigger. They were disgusted to see their living room changed into a butcher shop as the Russians dragged animals up the stairs to be killed on the carpet. They did not understand their persistence of using the bathtub for a toilet and the toilet for washing their faces. They could not help laughing over the disappointment of the Russian who washed his potatoes in the toilet bowl only to see them disappear as he pulled the lever. They saw with regret the wrecked automobiles and bicycles littering the streets, demonstrating the Russians' great love and little aptitude for things mechanical. They learned to know the Russian's great fear of his superiors: to make a misbehaving soldier run, it was only necessary to shout 'Commissar' at the top of one's lungs. They witnessed Russian soldiers marched off to prison, heavy ropes around their bodies, the point of the bayonet between their shoulder blades, like in an old war picture of a hundred years back. They experienced day by day the wide gulf that still separates the East from the West, as yet unbridgeable by any ideology, crossable only by armed forces, and haphazardly kept together by the permanence of terror.

Order was re-established in Berlin. Russian soldiers had been buried where they had fallen, on the sidewalks, in the centre of the streets. Their graves had been lovingly cared for. Little white fences had been placed around them. Flowers, and often the picture of the deceased, were planted on the heap of earth covering them. Their remains were now dug out to restore the streets to their original function and were placed into mass graves at more appropriate places. Barriers were placed on every important street corner. Smart Russian women in uniform, white gloves, their bosom pushed up to the neck, regulated traffic by lifting or lowering toll bars for vehicles and individuals alike. Like other regulations modelled on the Russian village, these traffic disturbances disappeared with the entry of the Allied troops.

With order restored, pillage was now directed from headquarters. The factories lost their machinery, the warehouses all they contained. Even the tracks of the city railway were removed, but had to be brought back at a later date. The streetcars were moved to Russia. The Germans repaired previously discarded ones; but they, too, were taken. Only the oldest, most dilapidated ones were left to Berlin.

With the entering of the Allied troops about half of Berlin was freed of the Russians. The expropriations were legalised, the removals were now being called reparations. The Russian troops moved into barracks and bunkers formerly housing German troops. Their uniforms seemed cleaner and they began to let their hair grow. But the more well-mannered they became, the less could be seen of them. Their isolation is not complete, of course; they can still be observed guarding the factories and offices that work for them. They have their parades and patrols and also their time off. They still plant their machine guns on railway stations to check the papers of all who pass. But there is no longer that one-sided 'fraternisation' of the first months of the occupation.

3

Russia has lost in Germany, most certainly in Berlin, notwithstanding all the apparent 'good will' the people show toward the Socialist Unity Party, Russia's German instrument. It is not propaganda, nor a stubborn refusal to be disillusioned, which explains some of the Berliners' 'enthusiasm' for Russia's German policy. Behind the 'enthusiasm' hides fear, which is kept alive by an invisible terror that may at any day come into the open.

On May Day 1948 there were nearly three-quarters of a million people in the *Lustgarten* demonstration called by the Russian-sponsored Socialist Unity Party. Apparently more than the number of those who attended the Socialist demonstration at the Reichstag building. Only two Russians in mufti, and one in uniform, shared the tribune with Pieck and his staff. Few Russians were seen along the route. The slogans were all related to imagined German needs, and against the Marshall Plan. Hour by hour the demonstrators passed the reviewing stand. Their shoutings, however, had no spontaneity, but were directed by groups of claques near the loudspeaker system. The Communist-controlled Berlin police formed part of the demonstration and received the loudest applause. Over and over again the loudspeakers burst forth with 'Long live the German people's police'. The Moscow-trained former Nazi officer, Markgraf, at that time Berlin's sole police president, smiled down to the masses, coquettishly waving a red carnation or clicking his heels in an earnest salute. Berlin's love for the police and the love of the police for the Berliners seemed boundless and all-embracing.

The shabby clothes, torn shoes, and hungry faces of the demonstrators made them appear like an army of desperate beggars, out to invade the reservoirs of the rich. But they yelled for the police, for the often-felt rubber truncheons, for the deadly order of the party-state. Did the bottle of schnapps they received this morning go to their heads? Of course not, for it was sold at once to the black market. The schnapps was not a present but cost more than a weekly wage; by selling it they realised a profit big enough to buy four loaves of bread. Maybe the sight of the large brown sausages sold at various booths near the marching-route made them love the world and all it contained? But taking the sausage meant to part with precious ration-coupons and to face a meatless month. No, the enthusiasm for the police, for the Communist Party, for Russia, was not the result of bribery; it was given absolutely free, it came from the heart, a heart obsessed by fear.

The manipulated demonstrations of the 'people's will' are organised through a malignant net of organisations. It is not up to the individual to decide whether or not to go. With others he is assembled at the place of work or at his living-quarters. His trade-union functionary, factory representative, party comrade, or house warden, will know if he missed the call, if he stayed away deliberately; and he may be reprimanded or reported. Reported to whom? That's just it. Under the Nazis it was clear, but now one doesn't really know. However, if the Russians should become the absolute rulers, it may be expected that a bad record or a deficiency of enthusiasm will reach the files of a new Gestapo. It is better to play safe, to act and talk as is expected, or not to talk, just nod, and follow the functionary.

Communist Party trustees, backed by the Red Army, control factories still working, supervise all available jobs whatever their nature, control the cooperatives and the municipal offices. Although rations are small, they must be bought. To live, one must work, even if most work is of the make-believe kind. Some jobs qualify for ration-card Two, others for ration-card Three, the most important jobs, as evaluated by the Russian occupiers, for ration-card One. To get a ration-card a work-card is needed. To keep the work-card, one must not oppose the policy and ideology of the Socialist Unity Party.

In opposition to the planned installation of a Western German government the Party called for a German referendum on the question of national unity. That no one is against unity is clear, though there may be some who do not care to show concern. That this is not a German question at all is also clear. What will happen in Germany and Berlin depends on the conflicts or agreements, between the great competing powers. Nevertheless, the propaganda offices are busy on both sides and the referendum is part of the Russian programme. And then it starts: – The house warden knocks on the door: 'Have you added your name to the list for the referendum?' He comes back next day with the same question, and the day thereafter. The question is asked at street corners, at the grocer's, in the factories and offices, everywhere, by a great number of unpaid functionaries in search of ration-card One, until everybody feels sure that he is watched, that his indifference will not remain unnoticed. The list of names demanding the referendum may be kept, checked, and gone over again, as soon as the Allied powers have left, on the day of reckoning when the unreliables are purged. Anyhow, it is not difficult to sign a name, and thus they sign – just in case.

Of course nobody is fooled by these expressions of the people's will. The Party is not gauging its ideological success but the amount of fear it has been able to inspire. By means of the referendum, demonstrations, elections, declarations of all sorts, it measures the degree of its power over the people. It knows that ideological control is of small importance in an age which has devaluated all ideologies, where ideologies are merely labels for the controlling powers of one or another set of politicians who base their rule not on ideas but on an effective organisation of terror.

Life in the Russian sector begins to resemble life under Nazi rule, including the arrests and disappearances of oppositionists in nightly raids. Although as yet without uniform and with restricted authority, a red 'SS' is in formation. Discipline and the leader principle are stressed, the party hierarchy and its system of privileges has returned. With the division of the people into ration-card categories an inexpensive army of functionaries and storm-troopers has been created. Being in possession of a number One ration-card means to keep on living; outside this category there is only slow starvation. The struggle for existence is a fight for the proper ration-card, for the privilege of being used as policeman, propagandist, informer, or executioner by the masters of the party-machine.

Russian expansion is based not on consent but on force. It is a military and police affair exclusively, notwithstanding all the doctrinaire concern with ideological issues, for these, too, perform police functions, leading, as they do, to the early discovery of deviations and nascent opposition. It is not the change in the economic structure the Russians may introduce in Germany that causes concern, but the political-social structure of their party-state. For the Berliners the 'Iron Curtain' hides no secrets. They have travelled across it, their relatives are living there, visiting them from time to time, either legally or illegally. Uncensored letters reach Berlin. They know that the conditions in city and country do not differ from the miserable conditions in the Western Zones, that Berlin merely reflects the whole of the territory that was once Germany. Furthermore, some of them have been with the Nazi armies in Russia, some returned as prisoners of war, looking like the inmates of Belsen and Buchenwald in their last stages of development. Local experiences are not their only criteria. But because of these experiences all that is Russian takes on a particularly sinister character.

The immediate situation, however, calls for duplicity. As long as there is a chance to pledge allegiance to the West, the chance is taken in the illusory hope that this may influence the decision of the Western powers to stay in Berlin. Simultaneously, the Russians are supported wherever necessary, in order not to arouse their wrath, in case the city should be theirs completely. As there are no escapes for the masses, their attitudes change with their masters. Democratic Berlin will be even more 'democratic' as soon as the basis for its current democracy – four power competition – is removed. Meanwhile, people can do no more than bewail their reluctance to follow suit at the first great exodus to the Western zones, at the earliest rumours of a possible Berlin crisis. Now they are trapped, to be sold out if so convenient, or to be used in a kind of test-case for the larger issues at stake. Those who do not live by politics will prefer to do as they are told, no matter who does the telling. The Western-oriented politicians will, at best, become refugees. In their majority they will probably crowd still more the already crowded Russian concentration camps. In any case, German preferences do not count; the present flood of brave slogans about the Berliners' valiant refusal to bow to the new dictatorship is only silly, facing, as Berlin does, an army judged able, in case of war, of overrunning the whole of Germany within a few days.

4

The political issues that seemingly agitate the Berliners only indicate their own impotence. Their interest in politics is waning. They would, no doubt, support any power, and any cause, in exchange for bread and security. They would even try to forget their early experiences with the Russians. But no bread and no security is forthcoming. It is the obvious poverty of the Russians, their strange primitiveness, their crude terroristic methods, their inability to give, and their need to take where hardly anything is left to take, that makes the Germans prefer the West. Even if nothing is to be expected from either side, still there is a greater familiarity with the Western world. There is also the strong suspicion that the Bolshevik colossus rests upon feet of clay and that, notwithstanding possible initial successes, it would not last in a prolonged war. It is not so much hunger for revenge, as the desire to escape the camp of the defeated, which motivates the German sympathies – such as they are – for the West.

However, no real turn to the West is possible. Victors behave as such; even where no great gains can be realised the victorious gestures will be maintained. These gestures alone confront the Berliners, removed as they are from the bargain-counter of international diplomacy, where special claims historically and otherwise, are framed in terms of coal and iron. France's anxiety over a possible German revival is not shared by her occupation troops, who recognise its baselessness merely by looking around. No fear-determined brutality accompanies their rule. Only the French officer behaves as arrogantly in Berlin as did the Nazi officer in Paris. And in the French desire to demonstrate their superiority the Germans may recognise their own behaviour of better days. It is not a wise girl who refuses a French soldier a dance in the Amusement Park; she may very well get her face slapped. One must be careful in the use of one's language when facing the French interrogator, since a real or imagined lack of respect may lead to painful consequences. In general, however, the French behave toward the Germans in Berlin as they would if they met them in Paris. In their persistent enmity they are like all the other Western people who endured the Nazi occupation. Apparently, they are not as yet finished with the war and their previously suffered humiliation still looks for compensation.

Only the British soldiers attempt to make themselves inconspicuous, provided they are sober, and so long as they are on their own. But they are forced to do a lot of marching and shouting. Their officers stick to themselves in Germany as once in India. Barbed wire around their compounds, toll gates, and many guards secure their isolation. They bring their wives and children to Berlin and live their English-way-of-life as if they were at home. The privates turn to German girls, which brings them into contact with the population. They are no longer feared but envied for their better food and happier outlook.

The presence of the French and British is largely ignored, however, as it is clear that only two great powers determine Berlin's status. America means many things to the Berliners. It means relatives and friendly organisations that send food and clothing. It means coffee and cigarettes on the black market. It means work and sales. It means a hamburger with a GI in the *Titania Palast*, and well-filled garbage cans for the scavengers. For some it provides the unfounded hope for social solidarity and for a turn away from the present trend of totalitarianism and war. For others it means effective opposition to the East and the certainty of war. For most, however, America is only the other side of the coin which, however thrown and however it will fall, spells doom for Europe in general and for Berlin in particular.

Although deeply involved in Germany and Berlin, the occupation army knows how to keep its distance from the defeated. The isolation of the Americans is perhaps even more complete than that of the British. They live their American way-of-life in heavily guarded compounds, comprising large territories in pleasant natural settings. They have their own churches, schools, and kindergartens; their own movies, concerts, lectures, restaurants, and stores. No German foot is to set there, except on missions of service. As distinct from the British, no program of austerity interferes with the Americans' pleasures. All less desirable activities are performed by Germans; Polish guards watch over them, their unbombed quarters are inaccessible to all but those with proper papers. Security has been developed both into a great art and a great science. To judge by the weapons displayed and by the red tape employed, the life of each American seems to be in constant danger. Even the *Fräuleins* need a 'social pass' attesting to their physical health, which was in former times required only of prostitutes. From another view however, all this isolation seems not at all queer, for it corresponds to the division of rich and poor that sets up barriers everywhere. The Americans in Berlin may be looked upon as a kind of new bourgeoisie, more sharply divided from the slum-dwellers than the bourgeoisie of old.

Of course, business closes the gap; the coffee from the States must be sold, valuables which escaped the Russians must be bought, and the requirements of the elevated social position demand a great amount of German labour. But work is fantastically cheap. Prior to the currency reform the weekly pay for any category of work did not exceed the German Mark equivalent of ten American cigarettes, that is four cents, as the PX sells the carton for eighty cents.

Nevertheless, the USA feeds part of Berlin. The Americans never tire of pointing to their deliveries and to the fact that they themselves manage without German-produced foods. Like the nation as a whole, so her citizens separately feel like philanthropists, the more to be admired since it is the former enemy they benefit. The hungry beggars have no choice but to be grateful, and their excessive submissiveness supports the conqueror's illusion of generosity. But there is no Jove for the Americans. The blockbusters are not forgotten. The Americans are preferred because of the crumbs that fall from their tables and because they are business-like people. They buy where others steal, they sell where others give. And even if the end-result – absolute impoverishment and complete exploitation – should be the same, the process to this end, in terms of personal experiences, seems not as terrible as the lawless past.

American generosity brings a bitter smile to the lips of the Berliner. He knows quite well what his rations are, and he knows the black-market prices. His bitterness on this point, however, does not differ from his feelings toward his own countrymen, the farmer for instance, or toward the Displaced Persons and the Western businessmen who are engaged in black-market activities. He cannot find any satisfaction in the thought that the black market must find its end as soon as Germany is emptied of all the valuables that still command a price on the world market, for he needs the black market and is by necessity a part of it. The temporary black-market depression in the wake of the currency reform did not help the Berliners much, as the 'cold war' prevented them from profiting by the farmers' and storekeepers' new confidence in the freshly printed money.

The smile released by the propaganda for democracy, however, has no bitterness at all. It can even turn into a hearty laugh if the question of the re-education of the Germans is raised. It is understood, to be sure, that an army is exempt from democracy, otherwise it could not be an army, and that an occupation army in particular cannot serve a lesson in democracy. It is rather the propaganda in newspaper, newsreel, and radio, that is found so amusing. Every word uttered in favour of democracy is at once contradicted by the facts of life. It is not the Nazi education of the past, having lost its dubious meaning long before the occupation, which explains the Berliners' obvious reluctance to take the dealers in democracy seriously; it is the close resemblance of their present life to that under the Nazi dictatorship. Of course they are supposed to pay for their sins of the past before being allowed to enjoy the fullness of the democratic life. The propaganda merely contains the promise of rewards for present-day good behaviour, just as the fleshpots of the Nazis had to be earned first by countless sacrifices and terrible suffering. But for too long the Berliners have lived on promises, and no longer do they trust in words. They are not cynical and disillusioned, as the observers say; they are merely sick of phrases totally unrelated to their actual situation. They do not see a choice between democracy and dictatorship but merely hope for the lowest possible degree of the terroristic rule of which they have had so much.

It is found increasingly difficult to oppose the Nazi observation that power alone determines who is to rule and live, and who is to be ruled and destroyed. The anti-Nazi cannot help feeling that authoritarianism has survived the Nazi rule and that the difference between oppressor and liberator is rather small. Hate and disgust grows, and dissipates into despair. It cannot lead to a revival of nationalism, as the material base for the latter has been bombed away. To get out of the country, rather than to revive it, is the dream of its ambitious people. They are no longer able, however, to feel embarrassment over the long Nazi dictatorship, and they no longer brood over the atrocities committed. They have grown cold to all but their own misery; and to tell them, as is often done, that they 'only got what they were asking for', causes no anger but only tired gestures of resignation. Whatever they were and whatever they have done, just now they only desire to live and to be left alone.

5

The desire to be left alone has nothing to do with the current issues of self-government, national unity, Western federation, constitutions, or the colour of flags. It simply means to be left out of all activities concerned with such matters. It is the desire to escape the manipulations of politicians, profiteers, and professional ideologists, and also the pressure of the enchanted minority defending traditional values. It is a vague longing for a new start, unaffected by the past, and an activity with no other issues than those of making bread and of eating it undisturbed. The desire is illusory but it indicates the prevailing state of mind. To be left alone implies also the wish to escape the war now in the making. The anti-war attitude is not based on theories but on direct experience in the bombed cities and on the battlefields of the world. They have learned to place life above all those considerations which are evoked in the justification of war. They are at any rate much too busy trying to keep alive, to be concerned with the larger problems of world politics. They do not really care about the changes of uniforms so long as they are able to use the night for sleep.

Sleep is important, undisturbed sleep of even greater importance, as the Berliners found out in the restless nights during the war. To go to bed with the careless assurance that they will rise again in the morning – this ordinary experience became the greatest desire of the bombed sleepwalkers. To sleep without the constant fear of death meant more than victory or defeat. Sleep is not just the mind and body at rest, it shortens the days, it helps against the cold, it is a substitute for food, preserves energy, and is the hiding place of misery.

Food is another of the Berliners' great obsessions, and sleep overcomes it only partly and temporarily. The individual awake is the personification of hunger. His mind is occupied with food and the question how to get it. All other thoughts are secondary and rather meaningless as long as the primary need remains unsatisfied. The rationed food is no problem. It is so little, and is sold at stable prices, so that anyone who works can pay for it. The only question it arouses is whether to eat it all at once or to distribute it over the larger part of the week. The answer depends on the individual's connections on the black market and on his ability to pay its prices.

The search for food goes on relentlessly, in and outside of Berlin. For food anything expendable will be exchanged. For a few pounds of potatoes great hardships are endured; hours of standing in line for a railway ticket; the brutal rush for a front place at the gate; the struggle for a place inside the train or even for hanging on its sides; the dodging of the police, and the long marches from farm to farm. Whoever cannot leave the city is busy visiting the grocery stores and black-market centres so as not to be late for the last delivery of bread or butter. They are always on the run for food, always asking for information about food, always excited about food, always thinking in terms of food, and all the while hungry to the bones.

There are many types of hunger, and the Berliners have experienced them all. There is the hunger for specific commodities that disappear in times of war. There is the desire for a balanced and pleasant diet, instead of stuffing the belly with whatever is on hand. There were the rations during the Hitler regime, which were seldom sufficient, and became hunger rations toward the end of the war. And then came the absolute hunger with the collapse of the distribution system during the siege of Berlin. To survive this period meant to eat whatever was found on the streets, in the ruins, and during frantic searches in abandoned stores. Wounded horses were ripped apart as soon as they had fallen. Most of the people turned butchers; like ant-heaps they hovered over the carcasses. They hunted for dogs and cats, picking from the asphalt what was red and bloody, even the innards of men blown to bits by artillery fire. Only to live through this ordeal, to be alive when the war was over, to enjoy once more a normal life, and to eat as much as one liked.

But the hunger remained; it was now organised and categorised. Former class divisions lost their meaning before the food commissions, only to have their illegal comeback on the black market. The law made new classifications in terms of ration-cards with different numbers of calories, dividing the population into groups that were to live and function, others that were to die off slowly, and still others destined to die quickly. The counting in calories may be good for the statistician and it may make easy the sociologist's comparative studies in living standards, but to the hungry it is merely the strangely expressed verdict determining their punishments down to the death sentence. But the judges are not fair, the sentences are not clear. What does it mean, for instance, to speak of the calories of ten pounds of potatoes if half of them are inedible, or of the calorie content of one pound of sugar if half of it consists of an undefinable dust? What does the rationed meat mean if week after week no meat at all reaches the market, or if it turns up in the form of ground intestines mixed with flour, or is substituted by a herring nobody knows how to fry for lack of fat?

Not even the highest ration covers human needs; it must be supplemented with black-market food and self-raised garden products. All other categories are only names for various starvation levels. They not only create new classes but also split the families into feuding units. The permanence of hunger makes sharing impossible. All sociality disappears; everyone holds on to his own, or tries to hold on. Some eat their rations fast, others slowly; envy and hate develop merely by watching people eat. Some men ruin their health quickly so that their children may eat, others starve their wives and children to retain their own strength. Suspicion rules, extras are kept secret, food is eaten in hiding, dragged into a corner to be devoured in animal fashion. People are nervous, ill-willed, ready to quarrel on the slightest pretext and more than often inclined to kill. Inequality within the setting of general want is the crudest form of inequality, the most corrupting, the ugliest, and the most vicious method of control.

If there were a sign that the hunger might end it would lose half of its terror. But the many years of repeated disappointments extinguished all hope. Even if the situation should change suddenly, the people would not believe in its permanence. They would merely eat themselves sick, would hoard what they could not get down, accumulate enormous quantities of food; it would take a long time before food would cease to be an obsession. Abundance, however, occurs only in their dreams; the recalling of the far-off past seems like a fairy-tale of well-being. Lucky are the children born into this misery. They do not know about other than the meagre rations, the substitutes, the skimmed milk if any, and the black dry bread. They do not know about candies, chocolates, and fruits, and often refuse these strange things if they are offered to them. The world of hunger, cold, and want is the only world they know about. With their toes blue in the sharp wind, they run about laughingly like other children. With their bare feet in wooden soles they play their games undisturbed. Their carefree attitude misleads the well-fed visitors to consider the claims of misery to be grossly exaggerated. The doctors know differently, of course; they measure, weigh, and keep records and offer proof that these children are not like other children, for they weigh less, grow to lesser heights, and die sooner when sick.

The older children are realists in the world of hunger. Their early life belonged to Adolf Hitler; no other ideas but those of the Nazis entered their minds. No one contradicted their childish empty talk. Theirs was the future – supposedly. And then all this collapsed. What was good became bad, what was once laudable was now cursed; if no one dared to oppose their childish arrogance, now no one seemed to care for them at all. They were either a burden, or a source for additional food, which they gathered by becoming small-time operators on the black market. Some no longer had parents; others who had, no longer cared for them. They needed help which no one could provide; so they tried to help themselves and sometimes they succeeded.

Disregarding the ever-present propaganda for the prevention of diseases, girls look for soldiers. They have been raped, why shouldn't they sell? What is all this talk about morals anyway? Of course, syphilis is not worth a pack of cigarettes. But neither is it good to be healthy and hungry. All is a gamble anyway, the good often die quicker than the bad. There is no love and no romance, it is all business on the barter level. There is little prostitution in the old sense of the word although there are still prostitutes around the *Alexanderplatz*. If enough buyers were at hand, prostitution would be general. Sex is a way of getting food as good as any other, and often the only way. The escapades of wife and daughter in search of food are disregarded; love completely disarmed, faces hunger.

The adolescents are frightfully realistic about the new relationship of hunger and love, of existence and sociality. No values other than material ones arouse their interest. They are practitioners of the empty life. The immediate personal gain in terms of things – edible, usable – is their only concern. Narrow-minded, without scruples, they turn their cold egotistical eyes upon the world of rubble in search for plunder left by the plunderers of yesterday. And since so little is left their selfishness is miserly; not even toward themselves do they know generosity. They calculate, count, ration, hoard, to secure their mere existence in spite of everything and everybody.

Hunger shows; it drives the smiles from the faces and tightens the skin on the bones. The flesh turns yellowish brown and eyes sink into their sockets.

There is an irritated tired look in the eyes, and sadness and anger around the mouth. The backs are bent and the steps are unsure as if in hesitation before the grave. When hunger comes, it appears publicly only in its early stages and in some cases not at all. Permanent hunger makes one indifferent, even to the self. The hungry hide like wounded animals in their caves. Starvation is not a street-sight; it doesn't offer itself to curious visitors. The people on the streets, and particularly on the still comfortable streets, frequented by the even more comfortable visitors, arc still struggling against starvation with all the weapons at their command. If they are hungry, they rush about not to get hungrier. They still care about their appearance, dress up brush, wash and mend not to add moral humiliation to the physical dilemma. The starving rush no longer. They do not clutter the streets; they have no shoes to walk in and no reason to be seen. They stay at home, in their rooms, live in their beds, or in the wards of hospitals, apathetically awaiting either a miracle or death.

Their peaceful withering away is the triumph of the rationing system. It is always a minority that succumbs first, to make room for another minority, recruited from the large mass of people lighting for their place in the majority. But in the end the various minorities represent a previous majority. This prospect, however, only intensifies the struggle for life and gives the hunger obsession first place in the minds of the obsessed.

CHAPTER 2

Authority and Democracy in the United States

Reflecting on the New Deal, Franklin Roosevelt once said that his government 'has done everything that Hitler has done, but by other means'. These other means, however, were not able to overcome the Great Depression which occasioned the large-scale governmental interventions in the American economy. It was finally only the resort to Hitlerian means – that is, participation in the imperialist war – which overcame the unrelenting crisis. Still, the internal situation in America differed greatly from those prevailing in the fascist nations. The United States remained democratic, not only ideologically, but also practically, with an absence of terroristic measures. A social consensus and an efficient prosecution of the war could be assured without much interference in the customary social and political institutions. To be sure, there were some violations of civil liberties such as the incarceration in concentration camps of Americans of Japanese extraction. But by and large the arbitrary discriminatory actions on the part of government were not comparable to the dictatorial policies of the totalitarian regimes. The manufactured mass hysteria of World War I reappeared, of course, but in a more subdued fashion. The actual outbreak of the war united interventionists and isolationists behind their war-happy government. The acquiescence of the population was obvious and in part based, no doubt, on the intuitive recognition that the war would bring the depression to an end.

Emerging out of economic crisis, fascism was an attempt to secure the threatened capitalist system by political and organisational means. These means were necessarily directed against the interests of the working class, in order to create the preconditions for new imperialistic adventures. This involved the destruction of the relative independence of the existing labour organisations, so as to establish that degree of class collaboration and national unity required for a political solution of the crisis at the expense of other nations. A repetition of the voluntary acceptance of the imperialist imperative by the labour movement, as during World War I, could not be expected under the prevailing crisis conditions, characterised as they were by an intensification of the class struggle. A new ideology, apparently directed against both the warring classes, had to be brought forth to transform class interests once again into national interests. This ideology could only be given practical form by way of political struggles, through the creation and growth of new organisations, which issued in the establishment of fascist dictatorships. In this sense, fascism expressed the capitalistic need for a total control of the working population, which seemingly could no longer be achieved within the confines of bourgeois democracy.

It was, and still is, the total absence of a class-oriented labour movement which helps to explain the persistence of democracy in America, even under conditions of great social stress. This absence finds its reasons in the particularities which have distinguished the development of capitalism in America from that in other capitalist countries. Although interrupted by crises and depressions, American capitalism unfolded progressively, until the United States became the most advanced and the strongest capitalist power. It became therewith less susceptible than others to the formation of anti-capitalist movements, for it proved able at the same time to accumulate capital rapidly and to improve the living standards of the great mass of its population. To a lesser extent, this was true also for the European nations, yet the very rise of capitalism there was accompanied by a far more intense exploitation and a greater misery of the working population than was the case in the United States. At any rate, the specific European conditions led to the formation of socialist ideologies and organisations, which persisted even after conditions began to improve.

We will not dwell here upon the rather complex reasons which hindered the development of socialist movements in the United States, but merely register the absence of such movements as a specific American characteristic. This is not contradicted by the sporadic appearance and disappearance of socialist and syndicalist organisations, which, at times, agitated both the bourgeoisie and the working class. These organisations did not represent the real aspirations of the mass of the working population, which was resigned to accept the capitalist system as its own. The only movement which achieved some social significance was trade-unionism: the utilisation of the labour market for the improvement of wages and working conditions within the – unchallenged – capitalist relations of production. It had no political ambitions but was happy with the conditions of democracy in its American form, that is, the two-party system, which provided no more than the semblance of democracy in its traditional European sense. Politics was left to the ruling class, as a matter of resolving those differences within the bourgeois camp which do not impinge upon its common needs. The illusion arose nonetheless that political frictions within the bourgeoisie provided a lever for the working class to affect policy by siding with either one or the other of the bourgeois parties. A kind of blackmail politics took the place of the political class struggle.

The lack of political initiative on the part of American labour, reflected in the apolitical nature of the trade and industrial unions, led to the complete ideological integration of these organisations into the capitalist system. Of course, just as capital competition continues within the general trend of its concentration and centralisation, so the fight between profits and wages goes on in spite of the apparent community of labour and capital. It is a struggle for shares of the social product brought forth by the capitalist system which both sides agree to uphold and to defend. The mass of the American workers does not object to the capitalist system, but merely to its pressure upon wages, caused, in their view, by the greediness of their employers rather than by the system as such. They are prepared to fight for the maintenance of once-reached living standards, or even for a larger share of the pie, but within – not against – the capitalist system. The wage struggles are carried on, often with great militancy, in the belief that the capitalist system is capable of doing justice to both labour and capital. And with a rapid rate of capital accumulation, implying the increasing productivity of labour, both profits and wages may rise, if only in unequal measure. It is then the experience of the past, which still determines the attitude of American labour with respect to the capitalist system.

Only a minority of American workers are unionised and the unions themselves vary greatly with respect to their bargaining power and the character of their bureaucracies. But all exclude effective control on the part of their membership; which is to say, the workers accept the unions in the same sense in which they accept American capitalism as a whole. With the legalisation and institutionalisation of the unions, which dates back to the New Deal of the Great Depression, 'organised labour' itself became a part of the system, confronting the workers as an objective reality outside their own control. Union dues are paid in the same spirit as taxes are paid, but there is neither a way to, nor as yet a demand to, participate in union affairs. Everything is left to the bureaucracies, just as politics is left to the bourgeoisie. In both cases the democratic forms are often maintained, of course, via elections and referenda, but they do not affect the authoritarian controls of either governments or unions. The personnel may change; the system remains the same.

The concentration and centralisation of capital in the United States has progressed to a point where the specific interests of the big corporations determine the destiny of the system as a whole. It was no joke when it was said that 'what is good for General Motors is good for America', for it does depend on the fortunes of General Motors, and on those of all the other similar corporations, whether the economy expands or contracts. In this situation, the state is the state of the corporations and depends on their profitability. Whatever differences may have existed between state and capital, they have since long been dissolved; the state is not a mere tool of the ruling class, the latter is also the state. It is for this reason that the people in government office, or any public office, need not be pressured by the big corporations to do their bidding; they do so on their own accord. Moreover, the personnel of state and capital are interchangeable; corporation managers enter government service, while state officials move into the management of corporations.

If government and capital are one and the same, this entity finds its support in the Senate and the House of Representatives. Democratically elected, the congressmen have been chosen to uphold the capitalist system and its state. They do so not only out of conviction, but also because of their direct capitalistic interests. As, according to Calvin Coolidge, 'the business of America is business', politics itself is seen as just another money-making enterprise, to be supplemented by branching out into other businesses, or by maintaining those already engaged in. The *New York Times* of 8 May 1978 reported a computerised study of the personal financial interests of almost all the members of Congress, which demonstrated that these people are also investors in all sorts of enterprises, often using their official positions to advance their business interests. As the information on which the study was based was supplied by the congressmen, the data were of course understatements serving to distract attention from or conceal their true but unascertainable financial holdings. For our purpose, however, the study substantiates the fact that the representatives of the people are also capitalists who secure their privileges through the democratic process.

The relegation of all decisive economic and political power to the hands of capital and its government has not as yet destroyed the myth of American democracy. People can vote, and those who vote – about half, or less, of the eligible population – can exchange a Democratic administration and presidency for a Republican administration and presidency; that is, they can exchange one set of people for another, equally determined to maintain the system which, in turn, determines the range of their own activities. Thus, although big business dominates the United States and cannot be dislodged short of destroying the capitalist system itself, it continues to dress its authoritarian rule in democratic garb. In fact, the more the ideology of democracy is nourished, the less bearing it has upon reality. Originally, political democracy was the goal of the emerging capitalist class and came to express the political aspects of capitalist competition, without ever concerning itself with the exploitative class relations upon which the whole capitalist edifice rests. In the European nations, the illusion nevertheless arose that bourgeois democracy could be utilised by the labouring class to alleviate its lot within the capitalist system and could, perhaps, even allow for the formation of socialistically inclined governments and thus extend democracy into the socio-economic sphere. In America, however, as we have seen, this illusion never arose, and the private property relations of capitalism remained generally sacrosanct. This has not changed despite the transformation of a dominantly competitive capitalism into that of the large corporation and the monopolisation of capital, which even precludes political democracy in the ordinary bourgeois sense of the term.

In America democracy begins and ends with the ballot box. But it is also perceived as involving free speech, free assembly, and freedom of the press. Generally, there is no interference with these civil liberties, for they are not made use of in opposition to the capitalist system. What opposition flares up from time to time demands improvements of the system, not its abolition, such as clean government, lower taxes, civil rights and, more recently, the protection of the environment. It is noteworthy that such demands are not raised by the workers but by the middle class, and express its particular frustrations. With their upward mobility increasingly restricted, and their unhappiness at submerging into the working class, they imagine the possibility of a well-functioning capitalism, capable of satisfying all social layers. They have taken up the opportunism and reformism which, in the European nations, transformed the character of the labour movement. Compared with the welfare ideology of the liberal part of the middle class, the American workers appear reactionary, by displaying no interest in social affairs except with regard to their wages. The opinions of the politically conscious elements of the middle class are therefore destined to be voices in the wilderness.

The kinds of politics carried on by elements of the middle class do not transcend the capitalist system. Even in their limited sense, they remain purely ideological, since there is no material force behind them. Still, as long as they are allowed to assert themselves, democracy appears as a reality with some effect on the course of events. This illusion supports the monolithic rule of capital. There is then no need to remove the democratic safeguard, even if this should prove inconvenient at times. In any case, it does not represent a danger that could not be met by the ordinary means of government oppression. The democratic forms are thus maintained as an asset rather than a liability of capitalistic rule, yet kept in bounds by the changing needs of the latter. This often leads to violence, based, on the one side, on the illusion that it is possible to divert the government from a particular course of action through the assertion of democratic rights, and, on the other side, on governmental assertion of authority in response to protest. Yet, after each such emergency, American democracy finds itself restored.

Any temporary abrogation of democratic rights is undertaken in the name of democracy, identified, as it is, with Americanism. Anything more than verbal opposition is at once branded an attack on democracy, which presumably reflects the general consensus. It is seen as Un-American because it goes beyond the prescribed, though ineffective, democratic rules, as they evolved in the United States. Being Un-American, it is perceived as a foreign implant, which could not possibly originate on American soil. While, at first, it was the unassimilated immigrants who were held responsible for all the unrest in the nation, later it was allegiance to social systems other than the American which supposedly carried the germ of discontent into the American fabric. To make the world 'safe for democracy' required then the simultaneous pursuit of the internal and of the external enemies of democracy and therefore of American capitalism. Even ordinary wage struggles were often denounced as the work of foreign agitators, bent on undermining American democracy. Despite the actual insignificance of these political currents, laws were passed against anarchism, syndicalism, and bolshevism. Even the democratic Socialist Party found itself outlawed during World War I; all in the name of American democracy. Fascism, were it to come to America, would not require popular participation as it did in Europe. It would most probably be called anti-fascism, as the American fascist Huey Long supposedly asserted, or simply 100 per cent Americanism. Without popular participation, there would also be no opposition; it would be a matter entirely of the government's decision. Repressive measures could be introduced within the framework of American democracy, preserving its forms while emptying them of all their content. The ruling class, in short, has managed to gain totalitarian control with precisely the instrumentalities that were supposed to curtail the monopolisation of power and the absolute rule of the capitalist oligarchy.

Class society implies the systematic manipulation of 'public opinion' as an instrument of class rule. The specific interests of the ruling class must be made to appear as the general interest. But in capitalism, ideas are also commodities, whose producers and dispensers find a market only in the ideological requirements of capitalism. It is therefore not surprising that the media of persuasion – the schools, the universities, the churches, the press, radio, and television, etc. – cater exclusively to the needs of the capitalist system. But where there is a market, there is also competition, and the ideologists may vary their wares to some extent, even though all of them have to serve the same purpose, namely, ideological support of the status quo. These variations on a single theme support the democratic illusions within the authoritarian conditions of American capitalism. The most reactionary ideas insist upon their compliance with the democratic ideal, even if this ideal refers to past conditions rather than to present-day reality.

Notwithstanding the conditions of monopoly, politics remains not only a business but a competitive business. This competition expresses itself in ideological terms. Although everyone agrees on the merits of American democracy, there is no agreement as how to serve it best. This makes for the subjective element in American politics, that is, the struggle of politicians to gain entry into the political institutions, or to increase their importance within them. The subjective strivings of the politicians becloud the fact of their objectively determined identical functions. But their antics are often topical enough to find a wide response, particularly if this suits governmental policies and specific capitalistic interests. Irrational assumptions become, at times, the reality of the day, as did, for instance, the Red Scare in the wake of World War I and McCarthyism during the cold war period. In the first case, a nationwide hunt for subversives was instigated as a kind of publicity stunt to further the presidential ambitions of the then Attorney General, A. Mitchell Palmer. At the same time, however, in the context of the Russian Revolution and its international repercussions, the fabrication of a threat to American capitalism could be used not only to ferret out an incipient radicalism but to subdue the working class as a whole. Similarly, McCarthyism, despite its source in the private political ambitions of its author, could spread as far as it did because it served the ideological requirements of American imperialism.

What is of interest in this context is the susceptibility of American democracy to the same type of demagoguery that created the mass hysteria and the fear of terror in the totalitarian nations. Only what has been, and remains, more or less the rule in these nations has been an exception in the United States. But it is an ever-ready possibility and another indication of the essentially authoritarian nature of American capitalism. A counterpart to the potential but mostly latent totalitarian tendency are the sporadic extra-legal outbreaks on the part of racial minorities, which strive for equality in a system based on exploitation and therewith on inequalities in all spheres of social life. They know from experience that democracy has nothing to do with their own conditions and offers no solution for their special problems. Still, they assume that the system could be forced to make some concessions by way of organised protests and direct actions justified in terms of prevailing democratic ideology. But this ideology does not stand in the way of applying the most naked authoritarian measures, if this should be deemed necessary. The apparatus of repression – the army, the national guard, the state-police, the local public and private police forces – are formidable enough to deal with such upheavals.

While the apparatus of repression is ever-ready, it can be held in reserve because of the overwhelmingly positive identification of the large mass of the population with the American system. This identification remains intact even when particular policies of the government are questioned or opposed, or when the government itself loses the confidence of large layers of society. The war in Vietnam, for example, was generally not recognised as an aspect of American imperialism, but was bewailed as a morally wrong policy, or as a mere mistake, on the part of the administrations involved in it, which assumedly could just as well have chosen another course of action to safeguard America's interests in Asia. But this war was fought in the name of democracy, to prevent the further spread of totalitarian regimes, and was therefore most heatedly defended in the beginning by the liberal-democratic and even 'socialist' elements in the United States. As far as the working class was concerned, insofar as its interests found articulation at all, it was satisfied with the war-given opportunity for secure jobs and higher wages. What opposition arose came from religious groups and pacifists, soon to be joined by a rebellious student movement unwilling to sacrifice careers and even life to the remote interests of American imperialism. Yet this movement used the phraseology of democracy to expose its actual absence at this particular occasion, and merely expressed the utopian quest for a real democracy, brought about by democratic means, within the conditions of American capitalism.

With all due respect to this anti-war movement, which did play a part in aiding the growth of aversion to the seemingly pointless extension and prolongation of the conflict, the war came to an end not in response to democratically exercised anti-war sentiments, but thanks to the defeat of the American armed forces, hastened by the war-weary attitudes of the field soldiers, who had lost all inclination to sacrifice their lives for the incomprehensible goal of defending American democracy in Southeast Asia. The fact that the war itself had become a commercial enterprise – not in the wider sense of serving the expansionary needs of American capitalism, but in the narrower, immediate, sense, of a general corruption on the part of the military and their advisers personally to enrich themselves – also aided this war-weariness. Finally, in conjunction with the then existing constellations of imperialist forces, the war could most probably be won only by risking a worldwide war, for which America was not prepared at this particular historical juncture. Capital itself brought the war to an end, apparently as a response to the opposition at home, but in reality because the expense of the war had lost all proportion with any conceivable future gain that might result from its successful conclusion.

Nonetheless, the ending of the war was celebrated as a reassertion of American democracy, as a sign of the power of the people as against that of the government, and even those who at first had endorsed the war as America's commitment to the principles of democracy, now joined the celebration. On the internal scene, a similar situation arose with Richard Nixon's forced abdication of the presidency in the wake of the so-called Watergate affair. A corrupt government was replaced by another corrupt government in a political power struggle lost by the Nixon administration. The ideological verbiage displayed in this process created the impression that, once again, democracy had succeeded in defeating its violators and that it was still a viable political system serving the national needs against the usurpation of power on the part of conscience-less politicians. Presumably, an aroused 'public opinion' had overcome the underhanded manipulations of the administration, out to secure its perpetuation in defiance of the 'fair play' of democracy. The euphoria created by this fresh sign of democratic power was such as to release a general onslaught against its various abuses, reaching the grotesque point of passing laws which subject the investigatory agencies of government to the scrutiny of their victims.

Whereas in other capitalist nations democratic institutions are increasingly supplemented by more direct administrative police measures, in the United States the instruments of repression have seemingly become more diluted, in favour of a more open and a more participatory political life, even though, or perhaps because, little advantage is taken thereof. It would be an error to assume that the hollowness of the democratic rituals is recognised and that the democratic ideology has spent itself. Quite generally, people continue to believe in this system as preferable to any other and express their patriotism in terms of American democracy. They are not distressed by its merely ideological nature; rather, it is precisely this reduction to ideology which allows for a persistent complacency of the American population under the authoritarian social conditions.

This complacency is nothing to be wondered at. The Great Depression of the 1930s is only vaguely remembered and then recalled as an act of God, from which no relevant conclusions can be drawn. Since this period, until recently, America was the toast of the world, the victor in war, and beneficiary of an unprecedented economic upswing which benefited both labour and capital. Theories were concocted which assured further economic growth and the elimination of the business cycle through state interventions in the laws of the market. True, there remained a residue of misery, particularly with respect to racial minorities, but this, too, would be overcome in time, thus demonstrating the superiority of the capitalist system in its American form. This general optimism created the various notions of 'post-capitalism', the new 'techno-structure', the 'end of ideology', and the coming of 'one-dimensional man', all signifying that whatever meagre expressions of discontent might arise would be absorbed in a truly integrated capitalist society without class conflicts, in which the difference between authority and democracy would have lost its meaning.

All this assumed, of course, the continuous expansion of American capital and therewith its extension on a global scale. The postwar situation was characterised not only by various attempts – some successful, others not – to contain the spread of totalitarian regimes in defence of the free world market, but also by capital exports on a lavish scale and the intensified creation of multinational corporations, mostly under the American flag. The internationalisation of capitalist production (in contrast to international trade) extended the American economy to all parts of the world, a fact of great importance with regard to the identification of American capitalism with political democracy. Business can flourish as well under authoritarian as under democratic conditions, so long as the authoritarianism restricts itself to political institutions. Business has no preferences in this respect, even though some businessmen may prefer one to the other. And in fact a great amount of American capital operates under authoritarian regimes and has a direct interest in their perpetuation as long as they secure and guarantee the profitability of their investments.

There are of course two major types of authoritarianism: the state-controlled systems, which imply the expropriation of private capital, whether foreign or native, and some form of central economic planning; and the various military dictatorships that abound in the capitalistically less developed countries dependent on the capitalist world market and the import of capital. Most of the so-called 'third world' countries are in this latter category, a condition described as 'neo-colonialism'. Here the authoritarian relations of capitalist production find their support in an authoritarian political structure, to assure the accumulation of capital, despite the precariousness of the general economic conditions in which world capitalism finds itself. The militarily secured rule in these nations merges the political elites with both the emerging native bourgeoisie and foreign capital, in this manner establishing the unity of capital and government which also characterises the advanced capitalist nations, although with a shift of emphasis from the civilian to the military aspects of capitalist rule.

Not admitting that American capitalism is based on the exploitation of labour – since each person is presumed to receive what he has contributed to the total social product – and thus sharing with the state-controlled totalitarian nations the notion of to 'each according to his work', the economic argument against such totalitarianism is largely based on the comparative efficiency of the 'free' and the 'regulated' economy, the latter supposedly demanding totalitarian controls and thus dictatorial rule. Democracy is then only mentioned as a political phenomenon, as a question of 'individual liberties' and 'human rights', which, however, are presupposed by the property rights of capitalism. With the private property rights maintained, even authoritarian regimes may develop, or return to, democratic institutions. In this sense, then, the various military dictatorships, particularly in the South American nations, are not opposed but cultivated by American capital, in the apologetic expectation that, sooner or later, they may adapt themselves to more democratic procedures. In fact, the dictatorships themselves pretend to be mere caretakers for democracy in times of social stress, eagerly awaiting the day of their displacement by viable elected governments and parliamentary rule.

The economic and so the political interests of American capitalism touch upon almost every part of the world. Although the nation-state persists, the economic integration of capitalism is international, which strengthens the imperialistic nature of capitalist competition. With respect to foreign capital investments alone, the Government *Survey of Current Business* of February 1977 showed that the yearly sales of majority-owned foreign affiliates of United States companies totalled more than $500 billion, while American exports totalled only $120 billion. No data is available for sales of foreign affiliates in which American companies have less than a majority interest, nor for the production of unaffiliated companies under licence of United States companies. If they were included, the enormous importance of foreign production relative to traditional exports would be even more evident. This implies, of course, that American capitalism must not be equated only with its democratic pretensions at home, but also with the authoritarian regimes under whose protection it exploits an increasing quantity of foreign labour. It thus shares responsibility for their undemocratic dictatorial policies.

It is true, of course, that American capital is not needed to foster authoritarian regimes in countries in which it does business; these nations adhere to dictatorial principles on their own accord. Most likely, the American capitalists would be more comfortable operating under circumstances more akin to their own. But they are also realists and accept the world as it is: democracy is not essential to the making of money. They are also quite ready to enlarge their capital under undemocratic conditions. So long as their investments are not endangered, the form of government which protects them is quite immaterial, and this indifference allows for adherence to the principle of non-intervention in the affairs of other nations. It is not the desire for a 'democratic world' which moves the policymakers, but merely the need for governments – dictatorial or not – that will protect capital investments and allow for international trade favourable to American capital.

However, investments are endangered politically as well as economically when a state of relative prosperity and social stability gives way, as at the present time, to a period of depression and social unrest. In such cases governments may invoke measures detrimental to American capital – up to the point of its nationalisation. If such events seem to be in the making, governments begin to matter and it becomes necessary to install ones willing to uphold American interests. Covert and overt American intervention will replace more democratically inclined governments with outspokenly authoritarian regimes, in order to secure both the specific American interests and the social relations on which they are based – as happened, for example, in Brazil, Guatemala, the Dominican Republic, Chile, etc., all in the name of democracy and the defence of the 'free world'.

But even apart from flagrant intervention, America dominates the economic and political life of her client nations through their financial dependence on the capital market. Just as the peonage of the landless peasant can be maintained by keeping him perpetually in debt to the landlord, so nations can be forced to submit to America's hegemony through their indebtedness to American banks and the American-dominated International Monetary Fund (IMF). If they cannot keep up the interest payments on their loans, which becomes increasingly difficult with the deepening of the worldwide depression, new loans are denied them unless they submit to a programme of 'austerity' designed to increase, with the profitability of capital, their ability to honour their financial obligations. The IMF has become the vehicle through which economic 'discipline' is imposed upon debtor nations in order to maintain, or restore, their creditworthiness. Of course, this is just 'good business', even though it may result in great social unrest and therewith lead to repressive measures of the most brutal kind. Recently, for example, Peru was placed under martial law, as its military government moved to halt a wave of looting and sabotage provoked by enormous price increases, instituted in order to reduce the payments deficit and to increase the rate of exports. In considering the nature of American capitalism, it is only prudent to include in its economic effects upon other nations also their political repercussions, which, in most cases, involve the application of terroristic measures by dictatorial governments against their impoverished populations. This, too, is part of American democracy, which works hand in glove with the authoritarian regimes, even with regard to the details of political repression via the machinations of the Central Intelligence Agency.

It is then not only the predilection on the part of American capital to assert its self-styled economic and moral superiority, as exemplified in its democratic institutions, but the inescapable need to assure its profitability under any and all circumstances, which turns it into an abettor of totalitarian regimes and authoritarian policies in the world at large. But the spreading economic crisis does not stop at the American door, and the same 'austerity' advocated abroad must also be applied at home. To be sure, the exceptional economic power of the United States does allow for a more gradual and less extensive reduction of living standards; yet it depends on the unforeseeable extension of the crisis whether or not the enforced 'austerity' turns into general misery as has been the case in previous depressions. At any rate, the apparent tranquillity of American democracy is steadily being undermined by the deepening crisis as well as by the attempts to cope with it, and the still imposing edifice rests upon shifting sand.

Thus far, however, no need has arisen to apply political measures to the economic ones, for there have been no political reactions to the deteriorating economic conditions. Unemployment and inflation have not as yet reached dimensions such as endanger the social peace. American democracy still reigns supreme and finds external reasons for its present economic plight in the unfair competition on the part of other nations, the pricing policies of the oil-producing countries, and the aggressiveness of competing imperialist powers. Insofar as internal reasons are added to the list of American difficulties, they concern, of course, the inflationary wages of organised labour, which are blamed for the lack of investment incentives. It is the gradual character of the economic decline which explains, at least in part, the apparent apathy of both the working population and the middle class despite the continuing reduction of their incomes. It also implies that the full burden of the depression is carried by a minority not large enough to articulate its grievances sufficiently to affect the broad majority, which still sees itself in an enviable position just because of the increasing misery outside their own living conditions.

However, the present-day lack of political awareness on the part of American labour, manifested in the undisturbed ideology of democracy, does not imply that the working class will not become restive with the worsening of the economic crisis. After all, it is the same working class which, although belatedly, reacted with considerable militancy to the Great Depression and finally forced capital and its government to relieve its misery through tradition-defying interventions in the economic mechanism. There has been no return to the pre-depression 'rugged individualism', and the American economy has adapted itself to a form of welfare system which blunts the social frictions associated with crisis conditions. It is then to be noted, as it has been by Professor Douglas A. Hibbs, of the Massachusetts Institute of Technology (as reported in the *New York Times* of 6 December 1976) that 'industrial conflict drops in rough relationship to the success of welfare-state policies in making government the instrument for allocating shares in the national product'. The Professor does not consider the limitations of these practices, nor the obvious fact that they must find an absolute barrier in the accumulation requirements of capital, which demand quite definite shares of the national product.

Should the crisis deepen, it will be somewhat more than wishful thinking to expect a change of attitude on the part of American labour toward the capitalist system, even though the direction this change may take remains indiscernible. Newly arising popular movements may very well sidetrack the aspirations of the working class into channels of activity that defeat their own purpose. On the other hand, the absence in America of capitalistically integrated and by now ossified 'left-wing' political parties may lead to the workers' self-assertion and new forms of organised activity more in keeping with their real needs. Moreover, the American crisis is a crisis of world capitalism and its general political repercussions will find a reflection in the United States. But as matters stand today, international capital may try once more to resolve its crisis by imperialistic means, thus pre-empting the possibility of revolutionary change in a new world war.

CHAPTER 3

Interview with Paul Mattick (1972)

Question
The parliamentary system of the West seems to be evolving in the direction of the pseudo-parliamentarianism that prevails in the state capitalism of the East.[1] The economic and political power of technocrats and bureaucrats in the capitalist countries continues to expand. Can we therefore consider the American 'Presidential Dictatorship',[2] of which even the opposition now speaks, to be symptomatic of the tendency within liberal parliamentary democracy to evolve into a new type of authoritarian and fascist system? The prevalent form of government worldwide, as United States Senator Fulbright continues to stress, is dictatorship. What is your view of these matters?

Paul Mattick
The 'Presidential Dictatorship' is neither a new phenomenon in the United States nor a dictatorship in the sense of the authoritarian states of the twentieth century. The American Constitution grants immense power to the president. Personality cults and respect for the state extend this power considerably beyond legal limits.

At the same time, politics is generally understood as a kind of business. The resulting cynicism presupposes a strong ideological glorification of state institutions, in particular the presidency. It also prompts aggressive political competition for government positions, often accompanied by all sorts of gimmicks. Like capitalism itself, politics as business results in an all-encompassing corruption of public life. Because the system itself is not yet being challenged, political interaction occurs by means of individuals. This gives the impression that politics and economics are determined by the ruling party and the president, even though that is not the case. This is why, for example, American domestic and foreign policy – from Roosevelt through to Nixon – remain unchanged. They are dependent on the overall developmental tendencies within capitalism and by the power constellations resulting from World War II.

---

[1] Editor's Note: The state-run systems in Russia, Eastern Europe, China, and parts of Asia.
[2] Editor's Note: The 'Presidential Dictatorship' referred to Richard Nixon.

From the workers' perspective, it is fully irrelevant whether the parliamentary system in the West becomes increasingly similar to the pseudo-parliamentarianism of the Eastern bloc. Neither situation pertains to productive relations as class relations, but to the usual illusion regarding accepted forms of political co-determination. With the birth of bourgeois society, the parliamentary system became a means to develop the capitalist economy and provided limited possibilities for social reform aimed at consolidating the rule of capital. The pseudo-parliamentarianism of state capitalist societies, on the other hand, serves only as a means of control for authoritarian state power.

During the rise as well as the decay of capitalism, the bourgeoisie is unified only in its opposition to the working class. Even under monopoly capitalism, competition prevents a unified approach by capital as is possible in the state capitalist systems. The unending processes of capital concentration and centralisation, processes that can never be fully completed, are accompanied by conflict in the political and parliamentary realms. Unless imposed from the outside, as in Eastern Europe, a full-blown state capitalism presupposes a social transformation. It is not an automatic outgrowth of capitalist development. The 'dictatorship' exerted in the United States merely expresses the hegemony of the most powerful sections of American capital, who also determine the general direction that political development takes. Even though imperialism is a vital necessity for capital, it pertains to the various sections of capital in different ways such that the general tendency must prevail against opposition. These contradictions within the bourgeois camp manifest themselves, for example, in the current split regarding the war in Indochina.

It doesn't make much sense to follow academic norms and speak of the economic and political power of the technocrats. We live in a capitalist society in which technology, like everything else, is subordinate to the accumulation of capital. Technology can only be developed insofar as it helps to extract unpaid labour power. Furthermore, it serves the political and military needs of imperialist competition, even though in this form it represents a burden on the production of profit. Technology relates to the immediate labour process, whereas the development of society is determined by class relations which in capitalism appear as 'economic relations'. Economic and political power resides in the hands of the owners of capital; the parasitic state apparatus is dependent upon the exploitation of workers mediated by capital. Under such conditions, technocrats do not enjoy a power of their own. They are partly capitalists themselves, partly employees of other capitalists, and in both functions bound to the reproduction of existing social relations.

When there is talk of the possibility of fascism in America, this is not about eventual developments as had played out, for example, in Italy and Germany, but simply about a more drastic deployment of the already existing means of repression. In the United States, a fascist mass mobilisation is still as unlikely as the emergence of a socialist mass movement. Aware of its weakness, the socialistically inclined population attempts to work within the framework of the given political institutions and does not constitute a direct threat to the ruling classes. Both 'right-wing' and 'left-wing' radicalism remain marginal phenomena that can be controlled with customary police measures. However, this says nothing about the future. With growing economic difficulties and the continuation of the [Vietnam] war, spontaneous movements may arise which necessitate repressive measures otherwise kept in reserve.[3] But conditions of civil war are nothing new in America; on the local level, they traverse the entirety of American history. State brutality in this regard is not inferior to that of any other country. In this sense, the present state can already be considered as 'fascist'.

Question
In the United States and other leading capitalist countries, the contradiction between public poverty and private wealth takes on life-threatening forms. In this context, liberal and socialist scientists warn that the destruction of the 'environment' will become irreversible in a few years. Are leftists correct when they argue that 'late capitalism' has entered its final stage?

Paul Mattick
Overexploitation and destruction of the environment accompanied the entirety of capitalist development. The longer capital rules the world, the more threatening these become. It is impossible to stop this process without also abolishing the capitalist mode of production. The moral outrage of liberal scientists and politicians about environmental destruction is a sign of either stupidity or hypocrisy, or both. For capital, only profit – the basis of its existence – is rational. Anything that poses an obstacle to profit cannot be taken into account.

This is not a contradiction between 'public poverty and private wealth', when the major form of 'public wealth' is an enormous expenditure for military equipment and war. Instead, this is about maintaining and increasing capital and its specific class relations. To stress environmental destruction as an argument against capitalism can only mean to demand reforms that preserve the environment for capitalism.

---

3 [Brackets added by editor].

Whether the destruction of the environment leads to the 'final phase' of capitalism is not a real consideration. The more recent manifestations of economic crises and imperialist conflicts show that every crisis of capital can lead to its end. The danger of atomic annihilation because of the absence of social revolution is much more probable than the ongoing destruction of the environment.

∴

There is no such thing as 'inhuman technology', since all technology is shaped and put to use by humans. Due to commodity fetishism, there exists in capitalism also a fetishism of technology, behind which lie hidden historically determined class and property relations. This itself implies that the fetishistic character of technology can be overcome by means of revolution. A social revolution would mean that science and technology lose the independent characteristics that appear as 'real' only in capitalism, and reveal themselves as human activity aimed at the achievement of consciously determined goals. It is not technology that dominates people, but technology as a means and manifestation of capitalist domination. We need not worry about technology, but instead eliminate capitalism in order to use technology in a manner appropriate to a socialist society.

Socialist democracy is only possible within a classless society, and it presupposes a social revolution. The revolution has nothing to do with democracy in the bourgeois sense, but instead represents an attempt to break the domination of one class by another. Only after the abolition of capital can a democracy of the working population in the widest sense serve as a basis to prevent a new authoritarian regime based on state capitalism. The council system in its original form seems adequate to fulfil the requirements of a workers' democracy, but only insofar as it is successful in preventing the emergence of a separate state apparatus. The construction and structure of a council system is partly a question of experimentation. To the extent that nothing stands in its way politically, only technical and organisational problems are at issue, which in principle are capable of being solved.

Question
What in your view differentiates state capitalism from a decentralised private capitalism? From the perspective of the working class, what are the advantages and disadvantages of these systems?

Paul Mattick
State capitalism so far has been that form of capitalist production relations that allowed underdeveloped countries to try to overcome in a relatively independent fashion their condition of backwardness and exploitation, despite the monopolistic control of the world market. They could not develop industrially by means of the competitive process, given the existence of the highly developed countries, except by an even greater concentration and centralisation of capital than that of monopoly capitalism. Capitalist monopoly in the developed countries brings about state monopoly in the underdeveloped ones. However, not all of them succeeded in combining national liberation with state capitalism. In many, a weaker version exists of the mixed economy of the developed countries; in other words, the dominance of private capital bolstered by state intervention.

From a capitalist point of view, state capitalism represents a different form of society than private capitalism, for the simple reason that it puts an end to the class rule of the capitalists by giving control over the conditions of production to the state, i.e. a different group of people. For the bourgeoisie that have been pushed aside, state capitalism is identical with socialism. Both systems preclude its rule. From the workers' standpoint, however, the relations of production have not changed. The workers still lack control over the means of production and the products of their own labour. They have merely exchanged one capitalistic relation for another. The state bureaucrats now personify capital, similar to how the capitalists did so before. What is needed is another social revolution to abolish wage-labour and bring production under the control of the producers.

For the workers, state capitalism is not socialism but a modified form of an exploitive society. State capitalism offers workers no advantages unless capitalist development is viewed as superior. It has an additional disadvantage, that is, struggle against the new authorities is even more difficult. In any case, state capitalism is neither a solution nor a transitional stage for workers in the developed capitalist countries. For them, the point is not to develop a proletariat and accumulate capital, but to abolish both capital and the proletariat. That does not change the fact that also in developed countries there are attempts to create state capitalist systems. One can only hope that, given the actual conditions in the state capitalist countries, workers will oppose these aspirations and substitute their own socialist goals in opposition.

Question
Since the decline of the protest movement against the Vietnam War, the press claims that a 'serious' left in the United States no longer exists.

Paul Mattick
So far there is no 'oppositional' workers' movement in America, even though we witness an increasingly critical attitude to the course of events. This attitude is also directed against the official policy of the unions – which represent the only noteworthy and yet questionable form of a workers' movement in the United States – and finds its voice in wildcat strikes. Primarily, this expresses a generalised and ever-more serious discontent with economic conditions and the war, which are viewed as related phenomena. This general discontent also extends to young workers and students as well as to the minorities who are hit hardest by the economic decline. What is called the 'left' here, i.e. the radical movement of blacks and students, like any hopeless cause, has no long-term prospects. It flares up and recedes according to a changing situation beyond its control, such as the protests against the renewed bombing of North Vietnam. Nonetheless, the media's talk about a decline of the protest movement is nothing but wishful thinking. As things are now, the near future will witness a sharpening of all social contradictions and with them an escalation of social unrest.

CHAPTER 4

Fascism and the Middle Class

Marx pointed out that at first the capitalist accumulation process leads only to a relative decline in the number of capitalists and in the number of workers employed; that, though both increase absolutely, their increase is slower than that of capital. All statistics on this point show that this development is true. Under conditions of dynamic capital expansion, the middle classes remain relatively stable; those of its members who shift into the bourgeoisie and the proletariat are replaced largely by capitalists and workers moving into the middle class.

In the course of capitalist accumulation, the relative independence of the middle classes disappears. The capitalisation of agriculture destroys the advantages of land monopoly. The increasing strength of capitalist industry through concentration and centralisation begins to exploit agriculture instead of being exploited by it. Middle class positions based on proprietorship fall under the control of organised merchant capital and larger industrial units. The power of banking capital falls victim to finance capital, i.e. the combination of banking and industrial capital. The necessity of transforming the middle classes into wage workers partly disappears when the income of the middle classes is reduced to wage levels.

The present plight of the independent middle classes illustrates quite well that they have been subordinated to the ruling class. That the old middle class has fallen victim to the capitalist accumulation process is widely admitted, for which reason the new middle class is brought into focus in order to disprove Marx's idea of the polarisation of society into two essential classes. 'Faster than the old petite bourgeoisie has gone out, the new petite bourgeoisie has come in .... [However,] the new petite bourgeoisie, despite its great growing importance in the conduct of modern industry and services, has at present very little influence over economic policy'.[1]

Economically this new middle class is in the position of the proletariat, for what characterises the latter as such is the alienation of its labour power from the means of production. Their existence then proves further that Marx's prediction as to the outcome of the accumulation process closely coincides with present-day reality, for he predicted nothing save that society will eventually be

---

1 Cole 1934, pp. 125, 127.

divided into a small number of owners of the means of production and a large majority of people without such property, and thus dependent upon the sale of their labour.

Though the ideology of the new middle class is anything but proletarian, the ideology of the great mass of workers also is non-proletarian. The ideology of all classes is that of the ruling class, and it cannot disappear unless capitalism breaks. The social position of the new middle class under conditions of stagnation and decline, a situation necessitating still further the growth of administrative positions to cope with newly arising social problems, lowers the level of existence for those groups of white-collar workers. 'The social level of the salaried employees sinks with the increasing extent of the group'.[2]

Precisely because the new middle class feels that it is driven towards actual proletarian living conditions, it turns against the present policies of the ruling class, no longer, however, attempting to arrest the capitalist development as did the old middle class but by fostering reforms of present-day society in favour of the new middle class. Because it attempts no more than to secure its wavering privileged position within existing society, it is not opposed to capitalism, but only to the capitalists unable to enlist and remunerate their services sufficiently. Their struggle is essentially a wage struggle, though this struggle proceeds by political means, as the economic power of this group is far below that of the industrial proletariat.

Under conditions precluding a decisive struggle between workers and capitalists, there is given to this middle stratum the possibility of playing a sort of balance-of-power policy. It can either tend to ally with the proletariat and thus force concessions for themselves from the bourgeoisie, or ally with the bourgeoisie and profit at the expense of the proletariat. This policy, however, finds its limitations in the actual status of the productive forces and their profitability.

The final outcome of capitalist accumulation, according to Marx and Engels, is 'a condition in which pauperism develops more rapidly than population and wealth. It becomes evident that the bourgeoisie is unfit to rule, because it is incompetent to secure an existence to its slave within his slavery, because it cannot help letting him sink into such a state that it has to feed him, instead of being fed by him'.[3] Under such conditions, the struggle increases between different layers of society for their share of the diminishing surplus-value.

---

2   Speier 1934, p. 116.
3   Marx and Engels 1848, p. 29.

The less the bourgeoisie has to offer, the more will the middle class tend to rely upon the working masses; it will be radicalised and will be ready to disturb or even replace the bourgeoisie. In countries where both bourgeoisie and proletariat are relatively weak, they may, with the help of all discontents, take power. In countries where bourgeoisie and workers are stronger, they may reform society, rapidly or slowly according to the strength of the different class forces. Then, instead of expropriating the bourgeoisie, they will rather share power with some of them, and sacrifice others, in order to be able to satisfy the workers temporarily and thus neutralise their strength. Or vice versa, the dominating capitalistic groups will sacrifice some of their privileges and destroy other capitalistic groups in order to establish complete control over the workers with the help of the new middle class. Or, to introduce still another alternative, a group of middle-class elements will, with the help of a particular capitalistic group or labour groups or both, forcibly displace another middle-class group and usurp their position. In short, the governmental changes are the result of class struggle within society which have their basis in shifts of economic forces.

It is their immediate interest as a privileged group in class society, and not any definite philosophy, that makes the middle class fascist, for these immediate interests can be secured only by way of political struggle for a greater share in the created profits, and therefore a struggle against all attempts to do away with profit production; in other words, a struggle against socialism. Where their immediate interests cannot be secured in any other manner than by a complete overthrow of the ruling class, they will proclaim their own elevation in society as the emancipation of all; they will try calling themselves socialists in order to rally the broad masses around them in their march to power and will endeavour to utilise their sacrifices in the field of production in order to stay in power. Thus, socialism becomes a new ideology concealing the continued exploitation.

The whole process in all its different forms actually means that the concentration and centralisation of economic and political power taking place during capitalist accumulation and proceeding faster during periods of stagnation and decline is now further accentuated by new political movements appearing under such terms as bolshevism and fascism. Apparently, this involves marxism in a contradiction, as the centralisation is more complete under bolshevism than under fascism, and more complete in the latter than under still democratic conditions. According to Marx, the more rapidly capital accumulates, the more expressed is its concentration and centralisation. And until the world war, it was actually a fact that the more highly developed capitalist countries were the more centralised.

In poorer capitalistic countries, the concentration of wealth had to be from the beginning identical with the concentration of political power. What was necessary here was not the slow development of capitalism by way of general competition, but a forced capitalisation necessitating from the beginning the most extensive state-interferences to compensate for the disadvantage of the tardy entrance on the stage of world competition. In other words, the high capital concentration of wealth already reached in the older capitalist countries accounts for the forced concentration of wealth and power in more backward countries. The Russian slogan, 'to reach and overreach' western capitalism, is not an empty one, but dictated by dire necessity, the necessity to avoid being exploited by foreign capital and thus hindered in national development, a condition which would mean to remain in the misery caused by the combination of general backwardness of productive forces and exploitation from abroad.

To change this type of misery into a capitalistic misery necessitates national-revolutionary methods directed against the vested interests bound to the backward conditions of the country and the interests of foreign capital. The capitalisation of such countries, then, when not accomplished by the still undeveloped bourgeoisie, must be accomplished against the bourgeoisie. From this point of view, the state-capitalist tendencies developing in both fascist and democratic nations indicate an actual economic weakness of capitalism. The forced concentration of all resources for an attempt to break the capitalist stagnation and prepare for the coming imperialist struggles explains, too, the forced polarisation of the society into a group of dictators and the great mass of their subjects.

The centralisation process cannot stop at national borders. The trend of capitalist development to reduce the number of exploiters, simultaneous to increasing their power over larger masses of exploited workers, forces international reorganisations of spheres of exploitation. The more limited competition becomes within nations, the sharper it becomes within the world economy. The essential method in this struggle for dominance is war. War presupposes an efficient war machinery and people ready to go to war. To prepare for external struggles, peace has to be established at home.

The bourgeoisie can no longer guarantee such peace with traditional methods. A new ideology is necessary, which, although it is intended to secure capitalism, is no longer strictly capitalistic. 'National-Socialism', the 'Corporative State', in countries already fascist, and 'People's Front' attempts in countries on the way to fascism, displace the old and discredited concepts based on a willing acceptance of class relations. The new middle class, unable to become bourgeois, unwilling to be reduced to mere proletarians, is best suited to, and actually does, create, spread, and defend the new ideology. Thus, this class basks in the spotlight of history shortly before the outbreak of the new world war.

In fascist counties, the new state bureaucracy cannot rule against both bourgeoisie and proletariat. To expropriate the bourgeoisie would mean to turn bolshevik and would lead to wars and civil wars in a number of countries. Under present world conditions, such a bolshevik revolution would promise anything but security for the fascist bureaucracy. In order to defeat the capitalists, the fascist bureaucracy would have to release proletarian forces too gigantic to permit the hope that they could be dammed again in the exclusive interest of this bureaucracy. On the other hand, living conditions of the workers cannot be reduced indefinitely, for at the point where this measure causes a reduction in the productivity of labour, it defeats itself.

In view of the impending war, workers cannot be starved. They must be put to work on armaments and fortifications, which no one can eat. The bureaucracy must disrupt more and more the capitalist mechanism, which it went forth to save. The senseless accumulation for the sake of accumulation finds now its climax in the feverish production for the sake of destruction. The fascist economy can succeed only as long as there is something left to be destroyed without destroying capitalism. Its whole economic policy, like all previous capitalist development, continuously transforms property relations, only more rapidly in the direction of greater centralisations of wealth – the more obvious polarisation of society into two essential classes.

From public works and armaments, it proceeds to the 'socialisation of investments'; from deficit financing to partial expropriation; from acting for capitalism to emptying society of capitalists. In this process, the state bureaucracy merges always more completely with capital – state and capital become one; and it makes no difference here if the people representing this unity consist of a larger or smaller number of parvenus, or a larger number of capitalists capable of adapting themselves to this change of affairs, or of profiting directly by it. Coming to power by a combined protest against further capital centralisation and against socialism, they are able, as soon as they begin to make actual policies, only to complete what capital began.

CHAPTER 5

Capitalism and Ecology: From the Decline of Capital to the Decline of the World

Nature is bounded historically by the second law of thermodynamics, discovered more than a hundred years ago by Carnot and Clausius, which foretells an increase in entropy that ends in heat death. Life on earth depends on a continuous supply of energy from solar radiation, which decreases however slowly with increasing entropy. The period of time for this is too indefinite and huge from a human perspective to be taken into practical consideration. Nevertheless, the law of entropy is always present and has a direct influence on the earth and on the fate of humankind. Apart from the sun, natural resources provide for the satisfaction of human energy needs. Their exploitation, however, hastens the transformation of 'free' into 'bound' energy, that is, energy no longer available for human use because of its decline into heat death. In other words, the available energy sources can only be utilised once. With their exhaustion, human life will come to an end long before the cooling of the sun, since the earth's natural resources contain the equivalent of less than two days' sunlight.

For humanity, therefore, the second law of thermodynamics is limited by the extent of natural wealth. The more slowly it is expended, the longer humanity can survive; the faster it is used, the sooner humanity reaches its end. Since consumption varies with the size of the population, the moment of global collapse coincides with the issue of population. In order to delay this collapse, population growth must be limited and the consumption of natural resources reduced. This issue has been raised by the Club of Rome in regards to the capitalist world. Wolfgang Harich now applies it to the communist world, since it too has been engaged in endless economic growth.[1]

About Harich, one can say: 'the leopard cannot change its spots'. His many years in Walter Ulbricht's prison never shook his spirit of opposition. If after 17 June 1953,[2] he turned against the Stalinist regime in the Democratic Republic of Germany[3] [East Germany or DDR] in the interest of the Democratic Republic itself, so today he turns against the ideology of growth in order to save the

---

1 Harich 1975.
2 Editor's Note: Anti-government protests in East Germany, characterised by public demonstrations and workplace councils.
3 [Brackets added by editor].

world by means of communism. Just as the DDR was supposed to evolve in the direction of the West after 1953 in order to solve its internal contradictions, so today the ecological problems created in the West should be tackled by the East in order to prevent the destruction of the world. For Harich, the abolition of capitalism is not only the goal of communist politics but also the only adequate means to return to a world without growth, on which depends the long-term survival of the human race. These ideas were posed in the interviews with Freimut Duve in the hope that they would avoid further misunderstandings within the DDR.

Neither Marx nor classical economics related their theories to the law of entropy, even though Malthus had introduced the issue of population into debate and Ricardo identified declining returns from agriculture as a limit to capitalist development. Problems specific to capitalism were explained away as natural and unalterable processes. These theories were developed at a time when agriculture still dominated and industrialisation was just beginning. Although production is determined by nature and human beings, Marx's and Engels's chief attention was directed not to natural limitations but to those due to the capitalist mode of production. The world – seen as nature – was still quite underpopulated, and the 'overpopulation' about which Malthus wrote, derived directly from the production of capital. Of course, an expanding population presupposes an increase in the productivity of labour, and this in turn presupposes alterations in the structure of society. 'The more I pursue this junk', Marx wrote Engels, 'the more convinced I become that agricultural reform and all this property nonsense related to it, is fundamental to the coming upheaval. Without that, Father Malthus proves to be correct'.[4]

In view of the dominant ideology of growth in the DDR that is intended to develop the productive forces beyond anything reached so far, Harich justifies his interest in ecology with references to Marx and Engels and to dialectical materialism. Referring to the French Communist G. Biolat, he maintains that 'the development of ecology corresponds to a new and deeply dialectical approach to the study of nature', such that his own concern 'is as orthodox as one can wish it to be'. Ecology refers to the 'reciprocal action between nature and society', which can only be fully comprehended by believers in 'the dialectics of nature' and the 'marxist theory of knowledge as refined by Lenin'.

The metabolism or mutual interaction between humans and nature has nothing to do with the dialectics of nature and is not disputed by anyone for whom the dialectic has no validity. Therefore, Lenin's epistemology is not

---

4 Karl Marx to Friedrich Engels, 14 August 1851.

required to discuss either the environment or threats to it, just as this epistemology, which Harich – to his regret – must recognise, has so far contributed little to the knowledge of ecological problems. In any case, the Club of Rome is indifferent to dialectical materialism. Likewise, it hardly matters for Harich whether ecological problems are subsumed within the dialectics of nature, an issue irrelevant to his diehard leninist orthodoxy. His argument rests not on the dialectics of nature but on the calculations of the Club of Rome, which start from the overly rapid consumption of natural resources and population explosion to predict the demise of humanity in the not-too-distant future.

There are aspects of nature that can be understood with formal logic and others which can only be grasped by means of a dialectical logic. Discoveries in microphysics require a complementary logic that is not identical with either formal or dialectical logic. The means to understand nature, including its effects on and relevance for human beings, provide no information about the 'totality' of nature and its laws of motion. Until now and possibly forever, these remain closed to us. In circumstances where a dialectical logic is required for the study of nature, we still cannot draw conclusions about the dialectics of nature, even though, in contrast, a society-wide dialectic is illuminated by economic development and the class antagonisms that result from it. It is, of course, possible to describe the law of entropy as 'dialectical', if only because it implies continuous qualitative alterations, especially when all economic and biological processes are traced back to their physical underpinnings. The second law of thermodynamics was discovered within the field of physical chemistry and not through a dialectical methodology. It is therefore proper to explain ecology from both biological and social perspectives.

Marxism is not a natural science and certainly not a science in the bourgeois sense, but nonetheless it uses scientific methods in order to discover the presuppositions and necessities of social transformation in general and the abolition of capitalism in particular, in order to intervene practically into social processes. Laws of nature cannot be changed; they have to be accepted, even though new understandings of them become a factor in human productivity and determine the possibilities for further social development. Those aspects of nature that affect human beings can only develop in a single direction, namely its decline. As long as this world exists, human problems will be determined by this world for as long as it exists, and therefore they must be dealt with within its confines. Even if it turns out that thermodynamics is only a peculiarity of an expanding universe and that in a contracting universe the opposite would occur in which matter could be created from radiation, this has no significance for a world that would have since disappeared, along with its inhabitants.

Even without reference to entropy, it is obvious that the exchange of energy between humanity and nature depends on the earth's fertility and the usefulness of its raw materials. With the exhaustion of the latter, the availability of energy declines along with the ability to intervene in natural processes. Marx and Engels lived at a time when the world did not recognise natural limits on production. Neither physical nor biological processes explained unfortunate social conditions. The exhaustion of the earth's wealth and the relative overpopulation were the direct result of production for profit and could be undone by the elimination of capitalist relations of production. One could not yet speak of an ecological crisis, in particular not from a marxist standpoint.

Are things different today? According to the Club of Rome and Harich, we are in the midst of an ecological crisis that obliges marxism to delve deeper into the environmental basis of society and the population question raised by Malthus. Harich believes that he can show how communist scientists, if not yet in the DDR, then in the USSR, 'are beginning to focus with greater insight on the ecological crisis'. To repeat: the problem can be summed up in three ideas – environmental overload, consumption of raw materials, overpopulation. For Harich, the solution lies in reversing these processes. This, however, implies the destruction of capitalist society and a revolutionary transformation on a global scale.

According to Harich, we are no longer dealing with a communist revolution as it was once imagined, in which society's productive powers are freed from the fetters of capitalist relations of production in order to meet ever-expanding needs. Counterpoised is Babeuf's idea to scale down productive forces and human needs in the sense of a pre-industrial ascetic collectivity. Marx had already emphasised that in capitalism the productive forces had become forces of destruction, 'and exactly this', says Harich, is what 'we are experiencing today'. This, however, is a misunderstanding on Harich's part. Notwithstanding the destructive side of capitalist development, Marx saw in communism the only possibility way for a further development of the productive forces which would eradicate capitalistically determined misery. Indeed, this assumes that the growth of society's productive capabilities no longer serve the chaotic and expansive needs of capital. Instead, they would be determined by rational human needs in conjunction with the technological and scientific character of any additional productive power.

This may turn out to be utopian, not only because of the prolonged existence of capitalism but also because of the limits set by nature to economic growth and not considered by Marx. The relative overpopulation that Marx wrote about has, according to Harich, become an absolute overpopulation. This cannot be overcome by means of a transformation from capitalism to communism, but only through a systematic reduction by means of population planning, not only in the 'Third World' but on a global scale. Even communism allows for no further development on the basis of modern industry, but requires economic planning without growth and possibly the liquidation of some types of production already in use.

In one respect, the ecological crisis discovered by the Club of Rome and others can be seen as a new attempt – similar to the efforts of Malthus and Ricardo – to explain social difficulties as the result of natural conditions, since to them this form of society appears to be natural and unchangeable. The novel element is that today there is agreement from the 'marxist' side, with either a good or a bad conscience. Of course, Harich's position differs from that of the Club of Rome. He remains aware that even with a full understanding of the crisis situation, the capitalist world is in no position to take measures to preserve human life for the distant future on even a more modest basis. The Club of Rome, Harich notes, indeed speaks of a probable impoverishment and destruction of the world, but 'it does not say that the rich must disappear from the picture'. People are indeed ready today 'to ration gasoline', but not prepared 'to ration everything'. But why shouldn't everything be rationed – and indeed on a socialist basis, asks Harich? 'Wouldn't that already be communism?' 'As a result of a rational distribution', wouldn't it be 'Babeuf's communism to which the workers' movement must revert. After all, it had reached a higher level by means of the dialectical negation of the negation after almost 200 years at the "source" of capitalist wealth?'

But why stop with Babeuf? Why not return to the perfect ecology of paradise before original sin? Babeuf had to fail because the one is as much an impossibility as the other. History cannot be reversed, not even through the 'negation of the negation'. A rational distribution presupposes productive forces that match the needs of four billion people[5] sufficiently, which means an expansive productive system that can counter the law of increasing entropy; in other words, a system that limits the expenditure of 'free' energy in order to maintain the negative entropy of the living world.

Besides, the rationing mentioned by Harich is not foreign to the capitalist world and has been implemented, at times more thoroughly than others, during wars (and also in 'war communism'[6]). In addition, capitalism is based on a type of 'rationing' that applies to working-class living conditions by means

---

5   Editor's Note: The earth's population at the time; it is now over 8 billion.
6   Editor's Note: A reference to Bolshevik economic policy following the Russian Revolution (1918–21).

of the law of surplus-value. This condition also characterises relations of production in the supposedly 'socialist' countries, even though surplus-value there appears as a surplus product. And actually, the existence of capital, as Harich himself explains, depends on a continuing 'rationalisation' of the labour force in order to satisfy the expansive surplus-value requirements of the accumulation process. Whenever necessary, capital will use political mechanisms in the attempt to reduce living standards to a lower level. Extensive global poverty is a product of surplus-value production, the result of capitalism's 'rationing' of life's preconditions for ever greater numbers of people, and for this reason cannot be endorsed as a solution to the ecological crisis. If it were a solution, capital would be well-situated to implement it.

When Harich speaks about the need to reduce production and consumption, the question arises: to whom is he speaking, actually? The workers, from whom more surplus-value is constantly extracted? The unemployed, who can hardly keep their heads above water? The hundreds of millions in the underdeveloped countries, who suffer from malnourishment and who are slowly (and often quickly) starving? If overpopulation and an overuse of raw materials cause such misery, a more just distribution cannot change anything essential. For Harich, accumulation must come to an end so that production covers consumption exclusively on the basis of simple reproduction and no population growth.

Capitalist production and property relations exclude the possibility of simple reproduction. An economic crisis and the misery that accompanies a depression set in whenever the pressure to develop industrially is suspended. If you assume that the ecological crisis is already underway, this becomes a welcomed situation. Nonetheless, without a revolutionary alternative, a crisis situation merely leads to a new period of accumulation. Simple reproduction is reserved for a communistic system. In Harich's conception, though, communism is not a possibility, even if the preconditions have already been established within the 'socialist countries'. Whether society can preserve its natural foundation depends on them and on the workers' movements in the capitalist countries. 'The overthrow of the bourgeoisie, the establishment of the dictatorship of the proletariat, and the realization of communism are', according to Harich, 'presuppositions for the aims of the Club of Rome'.

Apart from a handful of scientists, however, neither the authorities of the 'socialist countries' nor the workers of the capitalist world are conscious of this important task. As Freimut Duve emphasises, 'the economic policies of all nations – without exception – are the same as if the studies of the Club of Rome had never been conducted'. This is true for the 'socialist countries' as well, which nonetheless does not stop Harich from ascribing to them the possibility of a faster and better adaptation to the ecological crisis, as they are not subject to the pressure to expand. Since the destruction of the environment is a problem for industrial society generally, the possibility of coming to grips with this problem is in no way system-neutral. Unfortunately, the raw-materials resources of the 'socialist' countries render a communist revolution unnecessary. Eventually, though, they will also need to deal with the ecological crisis, since communists 'will never resign themselves to the idea that humanity is doomed to destruction'.

Meantime, it is a matter of once more swimming 'against the current' and holding up an image of the future, so as to indicate a means of escape. That the Club of Rome can only warn and make proposals, according to Harich, changes nothing in the 'revolutionary explosiveness' of the ecological understanding it has achieved. Even though the implications of this understanding can only be drawn by the workers' movement and the workers' states, they nonetheless require the revision of traditional communist conceptions. 'The advantages of socialism must be utilised in order to plan the production of all material goods, so that they conform optimally to ecological criteria'. To this end, says Harich, 'the left-wing parties must immediately begin to explain to the working class that as soon as it assumes power, economic growth must be halted and material restrictions imposed on the entire population, including the workers themselves'. This will be a revolution not for improving but for lowering the workers' standard of living.

It will be difficult to arouse much revolutionary enthusiasm for this project. This, however, is the least of Harich's worries. As a truth-loving person, he does not want to awaken illusions but instead make workers aware of the need for new sacrifices ('as popular as possible and as unpopular as is necessary given the judgment of science'). At a minimum, thoughts of prosperity and the fetishism of growth must be halted as much as possible 'by means of re-education and enlightening conviction, though also when necessary, by rigorous repression, perhaps by the shutdown of whole branches of production, accompanied by legally imposed but massive withdrawals'. It is clear, at least for Harich, 'that social ownership of the means of production, administered by the proletarian state, is the necessary precondition'. But this is not enough. The proletarian state must also have the power to control individual consumption according to criteria determined by ecology. 'Communist society must be established within a limited biosphere', Harich continues, 'one which will transform human society into a state of long-term equilibrium that limits individual freedom just as much as it sets limits on growth within capitalism and socialism. Any thought of a future withering away of the state is therefore illusory'.

This 'revision' of 'classical marxism-leninism' only targets the ideology but not the reality of the 'socialist' countries, which have never intended to renounce 'state authority and codified law' in order to actualise communism in the original marxian sense. Just as the authoritarian state, for Harich, was necessary in order to create with 'unparalleled harshness and brutality' the 'industrial foundation of national self-determination', it is even more necessary today in order to dismantle this foundation. Just as Stalin 'brutalised the country' for the purposes of industrial development, so must the proletarian state, guided by scientific forecasts, utilise all necessary means to force people into an ecologically compatible existence. Babeuf's communism cannot be left to the workers themselves, but can only be implemented through the inescapable state power exercised by marxist-leninist parties.

Duve objects that nothing can be said regarding communism from the perspective of Harich's authoritarian conceptions, since 'the management of scarcity bestows real power on the administrators'. The perpetuation of the state is naturally the perpetuation of class society and exploitative relations of production, which are at the same time relations of property. As state property, the means of production are still separated from the workers. Not the latter, but the state institutions which supposedly represent all of society, control how and what is produced. By means of the state, this society remains divided by a group of people who control the means of production and distribution and whose orders must be followed by the population. This new type of society characterised by state control of the means of production appears to the bourgeoisie as state socialism, or simply socialism. It, nonetheless, remains capitalistic in its relationship to the workers and finds a fitting expression in the concept of state capitalism, despite its self-presentation as socialism.

Once established, the reproduction process takes place as a reproduction of state domination. The growth of social wealth increases the power of the state. The international competition among nationally organised capital entities is sharpened further because of the differences between the various systems. Even more, social relations within state capitalism prompt the privileged classes to take a direct interest in the surplus product at their disposal. This means also an interest in the further development of the productive forces. These privileged classes cannot be expected to voluntarily set limits on their productive forces. Where forced to take such measures, these will not apply to themselves but will instead be imposed on the powerless, on the population in general. The ecological argument offers a good alibi.

These arguments are used by Harich to defend the backwardness of the 'socialist' countries in comparison to the industrialised nations. 'We must transform the West-East gradient of living standards', he says, 'which previously limited the progress of the proletarian revolution in the capitalist nations, into an East-West gradient of exemplary care for the environment, of a rational, moderate, and economical management of raw materials that results in a quality of socialist life in accordance with it'. Workers in the West, even if only after a successful revolution, are to take the lower standard of living of the East as a model and perceive their revolutionary duty in the renunciation of the few comforts which capitalism occasionally offers them. What concerns the workers of the DDR should be clear to those in the West 'that the characteristics of the DDR and the socialist camp in general, which we usually see as disadvantages, are advantages as soon as we measure them against the new standards of the ecological crisis'.

This inversion of existing priorities, despite Harich's imperative, cannot be achieved overnight. Babeuf's communism of equals presupposes a 'first socialist phase', as Marx already stressed and as exists in the DDR; that is, a distribution not according to need but according to work performed. Because performance is evaluated by the 'proletarian state', this state becomes the vehicle through which inequality is enforced. Its purpose consists of nothing other than this inequality and its own self-preservation. The new ruling class of the 'proletarian state' will as little give up its privileges as the ruling class within a capitalism based on private ownership. The 'socialist state' is no more able than its capitalist counterparts to heed the warnings of the Club of Rome à la Babeuf; instead, it acts at the expense of the workers, as is always the case with or without an ecological crisis. The working class of the capitalist countries is just as unprepared within the existing conditions of exploitation and inequality to set aside their own needs in order to preserve the environment as the workers of the 'socialist' countries are unprepared to renounce an improvement in living standards for the sake of 'future generations'. Class struggle, always latent, will be the arbiter of further economic development. If economic growth is to be halted, the class struggle must also be abolished. To use Harich's terminology, a 'dictatorship of the proletariat' led by the communist parties must be erected on a global basis in order to meet the demands of the ecological crisis, also in this 'first phase' of communism.

The class struggle cannot be halted by means of state power, but it can be dominated by one side for longer or shorter periods, that is, through a fascistic or democratic dictatorship of capital or through the 'dictatorship of the working class' in the 'marxist-leninist' sense. Whenever economic crises result from within the sphere of production, class antagonisms sharpen. This is true too for measures intended to overcome the ecological crisis, which actually correspond to the measures needed to overcome an economic crisis and which also can be expected to sharpen class conflicts. The ruling classes will respond to these ongoing threats and preserve their position of dominance, sometimes by dictatorial means and at other times by accommodating the demands of the workers in whatever ways possible. Privately-owned capital entities are only interested in measures that lead to a resumption of capital accumulation and an expansion of production. In order to preserve themselves, the ruling classes of the 'socialist' countries must increase the productivity of labour and expand production, and commit themselves to further growth without regard to the ecological consequences.

The warnings of the Club of Rome fall on deaf ears everywhere, especially in the 'socialist' countries where a new governmental 'bourgeoisie' has formed. This isn't an issue, as Harich imagines, of a lack of understanding by the 'communist' authorities, something that could be remedied by 'scientific' insight. The real problem is the class consciousness of a new ruling class that is no different from that of the old ruling class. The inability to distinguish socialism from state socialism, the only kind of 'socialism' that Harich can imagine, leads him to pin his ecological hopes on the perpetuation of a state dictatorship.

If the salvation of the world depends on the already existing 'socialist' countries and on similar ones still to come, all hope can be abandoned. Harich reproaches capitalism for its inability to halt economic growth; yet this is true as well for the state-capitalist systems that present themselves as 'socialism'. His illusionary demand for 'a stationary state for humanity within the natural world' presupposes the simultaneous overcoming of the capitalist and state-capitalist systems. This would require revolutionary movements which would not subordinate themselves unconditionally to the 'judgment of science' or the state. With deference to no other power, they would create a world according to their own necessities and needs.

Because such movements do not exist, we are stuck with the ecological crisis. 'Science' is not responsible for the use or non-use of its own results; this is left to the government and the ruling class. It is peculiar that Harich criticises the fetishism of growth in the name of science, since the latter is itself only an aspect of the fetishism of growth. Science is represented by people, not only scientists but also members of society. Specific social interests determine the range of applications for which science is used. The unfolding of capitalism's productive powers, or in effect its equivalent in the making of an 'ecological crisis', was a process made possible by science and its influence on technology. Harich now expects this same environmentally destructive science to provide guidelines for the re-establishment of an ecological equilibrium, whose practical effect will be to set limits on economic growth and also on the application of science itself. Indeed, he speaks about science under the 'dictatorship of the proletariat'. Since this is only another name for the perpetuation of the capital-worker relationship by means of government ownership, the development of science here too depends on further growth of the productive forces, whereby the socially determined interests of the scientists remain trapped by the fortunes of the state-capitalist system.

This is apparently contradicted by the recognition given to the Club of Rome by Russian scientists, as well as by the attention given generally to the Club's discoveries, which are credited with having a 'revolutionary explosive force'. It seems astonishing that this research has been financed by capitalist institutions and businesses such as the Volkswagen Foundation. Also surprising is the unexpected tolerance shown by the totalitarian states, who adopt pessimistic views regarding the future. Is this an example of a science that can function independently of its social environment, or are its present-day concerns also those of the ruling classes? Perhaps this has something to do with the need for long-term planning, or is it simply a last-minute reaction to a shortage of necessary raw materials and fuels, politically engineered by means of the price mechanism? Perhaps it is just a scam on the part of the scientific world, nothing more than a means to keep scientists employed and on the payroll through large-scale projects? Although the ecological problem actually exists, research about it has no practical impact. Whatever practical significance can be attributed to it remains contradictory. To the degree that the research frightens workers in both the East and the West into moderating their campaigns for improved living conditions, the result is an increase in surplus-value and surplus product along with continued ecological destruction.

Ecological equilibrium is an impossibility. The prolongation of human existence through the acceptance of limits set by nature is a possibility, but one whose realisation presupposes an end to the overexploitation of natural resources. These natural limits are in any case not yet the most important. What is necessary, now and in the future, is to end the human misery that results from capitalistic relations of production. This is the starting-point for a rationally planned mode of society in accord with natural conditions. It is one based not on further privations, but on a higher standard of living for everyone. This in turn depends on a decline in population growth and a further development of society's productive forces.

That environmental destruction is accelerating is not so much the result of productive forces that continue to expand, but results from the development of those forces under capitalistic conditions. Were capitalist production really what it is claimed to be, production for the satisfaction of human needs, the productive forces would have developed differently, with a different technology and different ecological consequences. Even with an enlarged productive apparatus, an expanding population, and new needs, this still would have been true. When the productive power of society develops by means of capitalistic relations and are tied to the production of capital, they can satisfy human needs only insofar as they coincide with the needs of the accumulation process. This precludes any direct reference to actual social needs and natural limits. Under conditions of capitalist competition – neither abolished by monopolies nor evaded by the state-capitalist systems due to their international ties – the productive forces develop blindly, especially as attempts are made on a national level to bring production under centralised control. This process occasions an enormous waste of human labour power and natural resources, which would not occur (at least not to the same degree) in another social system.

Although this wouldn't make much sense, one could calculate the extent to which the expansion of production is determined by the requirements of human existence versus the specific character of the capitalist mode of production. In other words: what would production look like without all the productive and unproductive activities required by capitalism? Surely such a calculation would show that at least half of capitalist production could be dispensed with without affecting people's living conditions. The larger portion of labour performed today is unproductive, and only makes 'sense' within the capitalist market and property relations. It could be converted into productive labour – 'productive' not in the sense of profitable but in terms of use-value production – while shortening labour-time. This form of production, because profit, competition, and the 'moral depreciation' of the means of production are eliminated, would bring about a meaningful savings of raw materials without compromising the production needed to meet human needs.

Such a transformation requires a social order different from the existing ones. According to the calculations of the Club of Rome, it may be that because of overpopulation, the limited productive potential of the earth, and the exhaustion of energy sources, we are already dealing with a lost opportunity. In view of world production today, we clearly cannot speak of an actual lack of material resources. To the contrary: despite the recent, engineered 'energy crisis',[7] the world seems to be suffering from an 'overproduction', or insufficient demand, as a result of a low rate of accumulation that itself sets limits to the expansion of production. This crisis situation cannot be traced to natural causes, but is based in the valorisation requirements of capital. Even for the Club of Rome, the effects of the ecological crisis will only become fully vis-

---

7 Editor's Note: Price hikes engineered by the Organization of Petroleum Exporting Countries (OPEC).

ible and take on catastrophic forms in 'two or three generations', and then only if nothing is done to counter it.

In the two reports cited by Harich that were produced for the Club of Rome, time still exists for the world, perhaps into the first half of the next century.[8] In the meantime, a way must be found to transform today's 'undifferentiated' growth into an 'organic' growth of the economy and society. The means will be discovered by computer models that project present-day trends into the future. Admittedly, this is about probable results, not certainties. While the first report on the 'limits to growth' concerned the world as a whole, the increase in total population, average per capita income, and so on, the second report emphasises that this sort of analysis precludes the possibility of a solution to these problems. The world consists of many different sectors, each of which requires special handling in terms of regional measures. If the first report warned that the world will break down in the middle of the next century, the second report focuses not on the breakdown of the entire system but on one or another of its regions, which would in turn shake the entire world deeply.

However it turns out, piecemeal or in toto, a breakdown is inevitable according to the computer models. It will be up to the 'statesmen' to save the day in a timely fashion. It is worthwhile pursuing the opinions of the Club of Rome's scientific experts, for example, M. Mesarovic and E. Pestel, who are responsible for the second report. They do not refer to capitalist society, but only to 'society', or simply 'humanity', as threatened by nature. From their perspective, the ecological crisis is caused by activities that 'arise from people's best intentions'. That these intentions involve the exploitation of the workers does not occur to them; to the contrary, they are convinced 'that the goal of reducing human labour by exploiting non-human energy sources is a project with which every person must agree'. They are unable to grasp that it is precisely increased exploitation of human labour that makes necessary the over-exploitation of natural resources. They have either no understanding of the society in which they live or they feign a lack of understanding in order not to be offensive. But looking at their proposed solutions, it is the first of these that seems correct.

These proposals amount to a series of noncommittal forms of talk, such as emphasising the necessity of a global solution of the ecological problem, a more balanced world economy through the simultaneous abolition of under- and over-development in the respective regions, an appropriate worldwide allocation of non-renewable raw materials and fuels, an effective population policy, a turn towards solar energy instead of more nuclear reactors, increased

---

8 Meadows 1972; Mesarovic and Pestel 1974.

support for poorer countries from the wealthier ones, and similar praiseworthy measures. Not a word is wasted on how this program might be implemented. What is certain is that the solution of the *problématique humaine* requires the closest cooperation on a global scale, since there can only be a future 'when history no longer, as earlier, is determined by individuals or social classes, but through the dedication of material resources to guarantee human existence'. This misunderstanding of capitalist reality is similar to Harich's misunderstanding of the 'socialist' world. In both cases, we are dealing with idle conjectures.

The authors of the second report almost seem to acknowledge that something isn't right. As 'rational' as the computer is, people are irrational. Although the computer demonstrates that people can be helped not through conflict but through cooperation, computer analysis necessarily deals only with the material limits of growth. The world, though, is threatened by people themselves on the basis of social, political, and organisational problems, which in the last analysis spring from 'human nature'. Since the Club of Rome is non-partisan with respect to politics, these problems can't be discussed politically. Nonetheless, it notes that the quickest road to the annihilation of humankind would certainly be an atomic war. Like the enormous waste of precious resources through armaments and militarism, this eventuality is not discussed by the Club of Rome, since the world is vulnerable to complete destruction even without an atomic war.

A dialectician like Harich cannot be satisfied with this. The distinction made by the Club of Rome between natural and social problems contradicts the 'interaction' between humanity and nature. For Harich, the possibility of an atomic war and the ecological crisis stand in a close connection. He does not deny that social contradictions trigger wars, but 'in a time in which economic growth comes up against unbreachable natural limits, we must also readjust our views. The ecological crisis intertwines natural and social factors in unprecedented ways …. The influence of society on nature can create a situation which then in turn drives society to seek refuge in a catastrophe'. It is therefore not enough to oppose war. The ecological crisis must be treated as a possible cause of war, in order to avoid war itself.

Nonetheless, there have been two world wars and many smaller skirmishes before ecological threats entered our consciousness. These wars happened not because nations fought – like dogs over a bone – about declining supplies of raw materials, but because the competitive struggle over the surplus-value extracted from the labouring population played out on a worldwide field. The competitive struggle exists under all circumstances, with or without shortages of raw materials, and thus has nothing to do with the latter but arises from the capitalist mode of production. Even when a shortage of raw materials and consumption goods lead to war instead of some other solution, this results from the form of society and not from the shortage as such. On this question, however, Harich again comes close to the Club of Rome's one-sided conception of the problem as purely ecological, without reference to the actual capitalist world. This world is for him too, despite the 'intertwining of natural and social factors', only a subordinate factor. Because an ecological crisis can lead to war, the avoidance of war presupposes solving the ecological crisis. War can break out at any time, but the ecologically induced catastrophe is not expected until the middle of the next century. It might be pre-empted by an atomic war, a ghastly demonstration of humanity's destruction not by nature but by capitalism.

But is there an actual ecological crisis? The numbers produced by the computer model to which Harich and the Club of Rome refer are open to doubt from many different points of view. Because the amount of raw materials and energy consumed by the industrial countries over the last 50 years can only be determined very inexactly, even less can be said about what is still available. And because we are dealing with unknown magnitudes, we can already anticipate frequent revisions in these estimates, not only through the discovery of new reserves, but also through improvements in the methods of estimation. To give only one example: coal reserves in the United States were estimated in 1969 at 3,000 billion tons; in 1975, this quantity was increased by 23 per cent through improved estimates. Whether too high or too low, such mistakes do not alter the actual consumption of raw materials and fuels, and consequently, it does not make much sense to counterpose optimistic expectations to pessimistic ones. What we can expect for the foreseeable future is that neither economic policy nor political decisions will be determined by ecological considerations, but – as always – by capital's immanent necessity for profit.

For Marx, capital has always created its own limits. The development of society's productive forces by way of capital accumulation not only requires non-renewable raw materials but also fosters a relative overpopulation, but in turn leads to the tendency of the rate of profit to fall in relation to the growing mass of capital. With this, the limits to capitalist expansion come into view. Even without the limits set by nature, capital must come to an end. Nature, consequently, is not the primary factor determining the relationship between nature and society. This hinges instead on the rate of profit as determined by the surplus-value and the accumulation process. The 'ecological' apprehensions of the Club of Rome, therefore, are often quite pedestrian, as was the case during the so-named oil crisis of 1973 – not a sudden lack of oil, but a politically motivated price increase in the aftermath of worldwide inflation that shifted the supply-and-demand relationship in favour of the oil producers. Left to the market mechanism, only a considerable drop in demand could affect the monopoly price, a result that would have come about difficultly and slowly. An increase in oil production, together with rising prices, would, according to the Club of Rome's second report, lead not only to an accelerated exhaustion of energy supplies but also to a transfer of wealth and economic power from the industrialised countries to the oil-producing states. Iran has already achieved minority control of the German Krupp Steel Works. Within ten years, the oil states, with an accumulated capital of 500 billion dollars, could take a large part of Western capital into their hands, thus shaking the world economy, inclusive of the underdeveloped countries, to the deepest level. Without going into these groundless and dubious speculations, it can be noted that the wishes of the Club of Rome for a 'global solution of the energy problem' derive more from an economic than from an ecological point of view. In any case, it is not an actual lack of natural resources that today threatens the world, but an unrestrained competitive war for global profit.

Because worldwide developments are determined by profit, the capitalists concern themselves with ecological problems only insofar as they affect profits. They have no interest in the destruction of the world; if it turns out that saving the world can be profitable, then the protection of the world will become a business – all the more because environmental destruction is a competitive factor for shares of the total profit. This problem appears in the economic literature under the heading of 'externality', the distinction between capitalist production and the accompanying environmental impact. Social phenomena are also ecological phenomena, for example, the emission of all sorts of pollutants which compromise nature and destroy the atmosphere's oxygen balance. Overexploitation is tied to environmental degradation, which is often assumed to be more urgent and dangerous than the rapid use of material resources. These widely known phenomena, which are attributable to the production of profit but also curtail profit production, affect the various capital entities differently and thus provoke attempts to limit the destruction. It depends on the mass of surplus-value whether these attempts can be successful, i.e. on an increased exploitation of the workers or on their 'modest standard of living'. On this point, Harich's proposals are at one with the measures recommended by capital, as expressed by the Club of Rome.

With sufficient surplus-value production, capital could avoid the destruction of the environment out of its own self-interest, although the cost would still be borne by the working population. Because accumulation sets limits to surplus-value, the ongoing destruction of the environment can be traced to the limits of the capitalist mode of production. As stated above, we are faced with a social, not an ecological, problem. But what about overpopulation? This is a real problem, one which will not simply vanish even with the possibility of a rational management of raw materials and an end to environmental destruction. The production of means of subsistence is declining in relation to an expanding population. Is the earth becoming less fertile? Or is it simply inadequate to support the growing population?

Among other studies, one undertaken three years ago for the Club of Rome under the leadership of H. Linnemann showed that the global capacity for food production has grown sufficiently to support a doubling of the population.[9] The current decline in agricultural production relative to a larger population has nothing to do with natural limits, but originates in social relations that prevent an extension of production. Similarly, world hunger has nothing to do with the productivity of agriculture. Even a doubling of production would not eliminate hunger; if anything, it would probably increase it even more. The existence of sufficient foodstuffs is no guarantee for the satisfaction of human needs. Commodities exist only for a demand backed by an ability to pay. For those who can't, overproduction can be even more dangerous than crop failures caused by nature. That crop failures can also lead to hunger has, of course, nothing to do with the unpredictability of nature. Rather, it results from the absence of measures, which in combination with increased agricultural production and improved agricultural productivity, could create sufficient reserves to offset natural catastrophes.

In large parts of the underdeveloped and predominately agrarian world, as for example in South Asia, it is not so much the miserliness of nature as it is a class system based on institutions and power relationships that prevent an expansion of production and productivity. Alongside the increasingly unsustainable subsistence economy, it is landed property, the tenant-farming system, usurious loan capital, the plantation economy, and the parasitical state bureaucracy that hinder any progressive development in order to maintain the existing social structure. The legacy of colonialism in the African states has meant a specialisation in the production of industrial raw materials which leaves them vulnerable to the miseries of the business cycle. Not only there, but also in the South American nations, industrialisation comes at the cost of agricultural production. Former exporting countries are becoming importers of foodstuffs. Russia's development into a competitive world power has required the relative neglect of agriculture, making the importation of food necessary whenever there is a bad harvest. The ever-widening discrepancy between industrial and agricultural production has less to do with population growth and declining

---

9   Editor's Note: Presumably this was the report later published as Linnemann 1979.

fertility of the soil than with the one-sided emphasis on industrial expansion and the growth of capital, as necessitated by capitalistically induced competition.

It is of course true that population has grown enormously. While medicine has lowered mortality figures considerably, the number of births has remained stable and thus appears as a 'population explosion'. It is also true that population cannot continue to grow and at some point will need to stabilise in relationship to ecological norms. This does not mean, however, that the current size of the population is responsible for world poverty. A level of production adequate to the needs of an expanding population would most likely show that it is too soon to speak of an absolute overpopulation. The proportional growth in agricultural production and productivity in countries like the United States and Australia exceeds by far the proportional increase in population. Although the same results cannot be achieved everywhere, even with the same methods, it is certainly still possible to increase the world's production of food significantly.

Only with an overall improvement in living conditions can a deliberate decline in population growth be expected. Of course, this can also be achieved through the use of state violence, so prized by Harich. Thus, in India at the moment, laws have been proposed mandating forced sterilisation, to be imposed on all families after their second child. From this it is only a small step to the direct extermination of surplus people. But there is also another possibility. Even if restricted until now to a minority of the world's population, the level of voluntary birth control in the developed countries demonstrates the possibility of population planning, which over time cannot only stabilise the population but even diminish it.

The warnings from Harich and the Club of Rome would be completely senseless were they not accompanied by the conviction that ecological catastrophe can be prevented. To admit this as a real possibility already acknowledges that it is society and not nature that will determine whether humanity still has a future before it. For Harich, the abolition of capitalist production is an essential precondition. Only in this manner can the ecological problem be addressed. What he has in mind is not a revolution that could lead to a communist society and therefore to a society that would be best positioned to deal with ecological problems. The Club of Rome cannot even imagine Harich's pseudo-revolution but relies on the good will and readiness of enlightened leaders to take the necessary measures. This is not to be expected, since these measures would also jettison the existing structure of society along with its representatives.

What, then, is to be done in this apparently hopeless situation? In general, nothing, so long as the problem is looked at from the standpoint of ecology. It is, first of all, not this that most threatens the continued existence of humankind. The 'ecological crisis' is largely a product of society's crisis conditions. This crisis precedes the ecological catastrophe. As things stand today, the likelihood of atomic war makes the concern with an ecological crisis superfluous. All attention needs to be focused on social processes that can pre-empt the atomic criminals of the East and West. If the workers of the world do not succeed in this, they will also not be able to confront the ecological threat in order to create a communist society that would make possible the further existence of humanity.

CHAPTER 6

New Essays

This series of publications, which appeared during the years 1934 to 1943 under the title *International Council Correspondence*, later to be renamed *Living Marxism* and, finally, *New Essays*, expressed the political ideas of a group of American workers concerned with the proletarian class struggle, the conditions of economic depression and worldwide war. Calling themselves council communists, the group was equally far removed from the traditional Socialist party, the new Communist party, and the various 'opposition' parties that these movements brought forth.[1] It rejected the ideologies and organisational concepts of the parties of the Second and Third Internationals, as well as those of the stillborn Fourth International. Based on marxist theory, the group adhered to the principle of working-class self-determination through the establishment of workers' councils for the capture of political power and the transformation of the capitalist into a socialist system of production and distribution. It could be regarded, therefore, only as a propaganda organisation advocating the self-rule of the working class. Because of the relative obscurity of this group and its ideas, it may be well to deal briefly with its antecedents.

Labour organisations tend to see in their steady growth and everyday activities the major ingredients of social change. It was, however, the unorganised mass of workers in the first of the twentieth-century revolutions that determined the character of the revolution and brought into being its own, new form of organisation in the spontaneously arising workers' and soldiers' councils. The council, or soviet, system of the Russian Revolution of 1905 disappeared with the crushing of the revolution, only to return in greater force in the Feb-

---

[1] Goldwater 1964, p. xi, states erroneously that council communists 'never affiliated with any major party', and that the 'great majority of its members were former members of the German *Sozialistische Arbeiter-Partei*.* However, council communism was the programme of the first West-European Communist parties before they were changed into parties of the Leninist type to fit them into the Third International. As regards the American group, none of its members had belonged to the *Sozialistische Arbeiter-Partei*, which held a position midway between social democracy and bolshevism. The few Germans in the American group came from the German council movement. The large majority were native workers, and those with a political background came either from the Industrial Workers of the World or from the left wing of the Proletarian Party – the most 'American' of the three Socialist groups that had vied for Russian acceptance as the 'official' Communist party. [*Editor's note: in later editions, the entry was corrected to the 'German *Kommunistische Arbeiter-Partei*'.]

ruary Revolution of 1917. It was these councils that inspired the formation of similar spontaneous organisations in the German Revolution of 1918 and, to a somewhat lesser extent, in the social upheavals in England, France, Italy, and Hungary. With the council system, a form of organisation arose that could lead and coordinate the self-activities of very broad masses for either limited ends or for revolutionary goals, and that could do so independently of, in opposition to, or in collaboration with existing labour organisations. Most of all, the rise of the council system proved that spontaneous activities need not dissipate in formless mass exertions, but could issue into organisational structures of a more than temporary nature.

In both Russia and Germany, the actual content of the revolution was not equal to its revolutionary form. Although in Russia it was mainly general objective unreadiness for a socialist transformation, in Germany it was the subjective unwillingness to institute socialism by revolutionary means that largely accounts for the failures of the council movement. The great mass of German workers mistook the political for a social revolution. The ideological and organisational strength of social democracy had left its mark; the socialisation of production was seen as a governmental concern, not as the task of the workers themselves. The workers' councils, which had made the revolution, abdicated in favour of political democracy. In Russia, the slogan 'All Power to the Soviets' had been advanced by the Bolsheviks for tactical and opportunistic reasons. Once in power, however, the Bolshevik government dismantled the soviet system to secure its own authoritarian rule. The Russian soviets proved unable to forestall the transformation of the soviet into a party dictatorship.

It is clear that workers' self-organisation is no guarantee against policies and actions contrary to proletarian class interests. In that case, however, they are superseded by traditional or new forms of control, by the old or newly established authorities. Unless spontaneous movements, issuing into organisational forms of proletarian self-determination, usurp control over society and therewith over their own lives, they are bound to disappear again into the anonymity of mere potentiality. This is not true, of course, for the minority of conscious revolutionaries who expect and prepare for new social struggles and to that end concern themselves not only with the critique of capitalist society but also with the criticism of the means required to put an end to it.

This accounts for the left opposition within the communist movement, which arose as early as 1918 and directed itself against the opportunism of the Bolshevik Party in its endeavour to secure the existence of the Bolshevik government. Although bad experiences with bourgeois parliamentarianism and with the class-collaborationist practices of trade unionism had turned Western communists into antiparliamentarians and anti-trade unionists, and thus into supporters of the council movement, the Bolsheviks insisted on a reversal of policies and the return to parliamentarianism and trade unionism. The communist parties were split and their left wings excluded from the Communist International. Lenin's pamphlet, *Radicalism, an Infantile Disease of Communism* (1920),[2] was written to destroy the influence of the *Left* in Western Europe.

With the prestige of success on their side, and with the material means available to government to influence or destroy rival social movements, the Bolsheviks succeeded in reducing left communism to practical insignificance. But it was never completely extinguished and has continued to exist in small groups in a number of countries down to the present day. For a time, it even won a hearing in the United States, where the lack of revolutionary conditions condemned communism to exist in merely ideological form. The formation of groups of council communists was first made possible here during the Great Depression, which saw the spontaneous growth of organisations of the jobless and of councils of the unemployed.

With the demise of the unemployed movement, the group of council communists elected to continue to function as an educational organisation. A split in the Proletarian Party added to their membership and made possible the publication of *Council Correspondence*. At the founding of the group, it adopted the temporary name United Workers Party, soon to be changed to council communists. It was, perhaps, due to the character of the group and its intentions that it failed to attract intellectuals into its ranks. With the exception of articles translated from European sources, all the material published in *Council Correspondence* was written by employed or unemployed workers. Contributions were not signed because they expressed the opinions of the group even when written by individuals. There was, of course, no money available to pay for printing, and the magazine was produced by voluntary labour. Only with an increase in the number of readers, which coincided with a membership decline in the group, did it become both possible and necessary to print the journal. In view of the reduced membership, however, it was clear that *Council Correspondence* did not promote the growth of the organisation but was practically no more than a vehicle for the elucidation of the ideas of council communism. For this reason, the change of name to *Living Marxism* was decided upon. Eventually, however, the general decline of radicalism resulting from America's entry into World War II made the name *Living Marxism* seem rather pretentious, as

---

2   [Editor's note: Mattick's title is taken from the German pamphlet of 1920; in English, it has been printed as: *'Left-Wing' Communism: An Infantile Disorder*.]

well as a hindrance in the search for a wider circulation. It was changed to *New Essays*, but this did not yield the hoped-for results. After a few issues it became clear that a sufficient number of subscribers to make the magazine financially viable was not forthcoming.

Throughout the existence of *International Council Correspondence*, no attempt was made to simplify its style or content to suit less-educated workers. The intention was to raise their level of understanding and to acquaint them with the complexities of social, economic, and political issues. The magazine was also written for politically advanced workers and for the council communists themselves so as to improve the collective knowledge of the group. It was a forum for discussion, unhampered by any specific dogmatic point of view, and open to new ideas that had some relevance to the council movement. The magazine eventually succeeded in attracting contributions from socialist writers who were not associated with the group. And it had, of course, at its disposal the work of some academic people, for instance. Anton Pannekoek (writing under the pseudonym J. Harper), an advocate of workers' councils since their very inception. Others, like Otto Rühle, had been active in workers' councils during the German revolution. It was Karl Korsch, however, who became *Living Marxism*'s most prominent academic contributor as well as theoretician of the council movement.

Because large-scale unemployment was the most important aspect of the depression years, it received special attention in *Council Correspondence* – particularly with regard to self-help organisations and direct actions that attempted to alleviate the miseries of the unemployed. Connected with this in a special sense, but also for general reasons, was a great concern with the inherent contradictions of the capitalist system and their unfolding in the course of its development. The nature of capitalist crisis was more intensely discussed, and on a higher theoretical level, than is generally the rule in labour publications, encompassing as it did the most recent interpretations of marxist economic theory and its application to prevailing conditions. The various articles devoted to this subject make their perusal highly rewarding even today, since they have lost neither their actuality nor their validity.

In political terms, the, rising tide of fascism, and thus the certainty of a new world war, occupied most of the space in *Council Correspondence* – not only with regard to the European scene but also with respect to its interconnections with Asia and the United States. From its earliest beginnings, German National-Socialism was recognised as preparation for a war to redivide economic power on a worldwide scale favouring German capitalism. The reactions to fascist imperialism were considered as being equally determined by competitive capitalist interests. Fascism and war were seen as directed against the international working class, for both attempted to solve the crisis by capitalistic means in order to sustain the capitalist system as such.

The anti-fascist civil war in Spain, which was immediately a proving ground for World War II, found the council communists quite naturally – despite their marxist orientation – on the side of the anarcho-syndicalists, even though circumstances compelled the latter to sacrifice their own principles to the protracted struggle against the common fascist enemy. The essays devoted to the civil war were of a critical nature and for that reason possessed a high degree of objectivity, which made the failure of anti-fascism – as a mere political movement – more explicit. Not only were the political-military struggles, foreign interventions, and frictions within the anti-fascist camp adequately dealt with, but even more attention was given to the short-lived collectivisation of industry and agriculture in the anarchist-dominated centres of revolutionary Spain.

Insofar as the problem of the collective economy has been dealt with at all in nineteenth-century socialist literature, it was in terms of the nationalisation of productive resources and government control of production and distribution. Only with the Russian Revolution did this problem assume actual importance, even though the socioeconomic conditions in Russia allowed for no more than a state-controlled economy that retained all the essential economic categories of capital production. This system may best be described as state capitalism. In spite of its differences from the capitalism of old, it was, as far as the working class was concerned, merely another system of capitalist exploitation. The council movement did not recognise its planned economy as either a socialist economy or a transition to such an economy, and opposed it not merely by denunciation but by developing its own concept of a socialist society as a free association of producers in full command of all decisioning power connected with the production and distribution process.

The organisation of socialism was, then, a recurrent theme in *Council Correspondence* and *Living Marxism*, for the questions it raised could be answered neither by the localised collectivisation of economically backward Spain nor by the centralised government planning in equally economically backward Russia. Quite generally, however, Russia's state capitalism was either bewailed or celebrated as the realisation of socialism – or, at any rate, as the road leading to it – and this illusion, though aiding Russian state interests, was detrimental to the international labour movement. It was the function of council communism, through its publications, to aid in the destruction of this illusion. There was no longer an urgent need to oppose social democracy. It had already, through its own practices, demonstrated its non-socialist character and was now in the process of shedding its socialist ideology as well. This, however, gave the no less counterrevolutionary activities of international bolshevism an unwarranted nimbus. Much space was, therefore, given to analyses of both the theory and practice of bolshevism, going back to its earliest critics, such as Rosa Luxemburg, and bringing this criticism forward by following the history of bolshevism down to World War II. This criticism was all-inclusive, philosophical, political, economic, and organisational, and expressed at an early date what became, only much later, a more widely accepted recognition of the true nature of bolshevism.

Criticism of the old labour movement, whether reformist or revolutionary in its tactics, did not exhaust the repertoire of *Council Correspondence*. Many of its articles and essays dealt with issues of a scholarly nature of more general interest, ranging from problems of psychology, sociology, and literature to such items as geopolitics, nationalism, and imperialism. Quite a number of these essays have been steadily reprinted by other publications and have served different authors as material for their own productions. Yet, for some years after World War II, the ideas propounded in the publications of council communism seemed to be totally lost. Since then, however, a new interest in workers' councils has brought into being a great international library devoted to the subject and its history. This new interest was undoubtedly fostered by the institutionalisation of workers' councils, shop stewards, and workers' committees in almost all the West European nations, by the rather emasculated workers' councils in the Yugoslav market socialism, and, last but not least, by their emergence as revolutionary organisations in the recent social upheavals in communist Poland and Hungary. In view of this situation, this reprint of *International Council Correspondence* and its successors is not only of historical interest but may, in a small way, throw some light on the potentialities of a future labour movement.

CHAPTER 7

Dynamics of the Mixed Economy

1

The theory of the 'mixed' or 'dual' economy is Keynesian. This type of economy, implying government monetary and fiscal intervention in the market mechanism, is still very much with us; but its theory, or ideology, is in crisis. Quite frequently the question is raised whether or not Keynesian economics is 'outdated', and demands are heard for either a 'meta-Keynesian' approach to economic problems or for replacing the 'conservative' with a more 'radical' version of Keynesianism. These laments are not the outcome of any recently noticed internal inconsistencies in Keynes's theory but of the relative stagnation of the mixed economy and its apparent inability to solve the problems of adequate investment and employment. To find an answer to the question of what went wrong, it will be useful to deal briefly with the rise and early success of the Keynesian economy.

Keynes, being a kind of neo-mercantilist, was fully aware that government has always had a hand in the national economy. It was merely a question of more or less, and *laissez-faire* meant less. War and revolution, however, brought with them increasing government control. Keynes's *General Theory of Employment, Interest and Money* was a reaction to the 'war socialism' practised by governments of the warring nations during the First World War, to the Bolshevik 'experiment' in state ownership, and to crisis conditions in the wake of the war which became worldwide with the collapse of America's prosperity in 1929. After that, unemployment was the great social problem and its immediate cause was recognised in a general decline of investments. It occurred to Keynes that the problem could be solved through appropriate government measures.

Whatever the explanation for the lack of investment and ensuing unemployment, it seemed necessary to increase the former in order to end the latter. For Keynes, investment was an act of future consumption, and consumption itself the end of all economic activity. He found that, due to a 'psychological law', consumption as a percentage of income decreases with economic expansion, and that in a 'mature' society the 'propensity to consume' is too weak to bring forth an 'effective demand' able to secure full employment. But ways were still open to increase economic activity through government-induced production and consumption.

To increase production through investment, the inducement to invest must be stimulated by greater profitability through lower interest rates and, perhaps, monetary inflation. To raise the propensity to consume, public works and welfare policies are required. Idle money could be borrowed by governments for financing public undertakings that exceeded their taxing capacities. Deficit financing did not really contradict the prevalent notion that a balanced budget was necessary. There was no need to achieve a balance annually; the surpluses of prosperous years could compensate for deficits acquired in depression years. The theory of the centrally and consciously stabilised economy reduced itself, finally, to *techniques* of income distribution – affecting both the present and the future – by which a state of unemployment could be changed into one of full employment.

Inflation, deficit financing, and public works have, of course, been applied in times long past but without the theoretical embroidery provided by Keynes. They were not only independent of Keynes's particular reasoning but their effects were 'reversible' and they could be employed for ends different from those suggested by Keynes. Indeed, Keynes himself found that fiscal and monetary manipulation could be used for decreasing instead of increasing the 'propensity to consume' and for increasing instead of decreasing 'savings' in order to finance such large public undertakings as the Second World War. In this 'inverted' form, Keynesianism proved to be a full 'success' in contrast to its 'failure' during the preceding depression years.

Aside from the factor of ideology, it is now generally acknowledged that it is a function of government to maintain a socially satisfactory level of economic activity. Little doubt is displayed that government intervention in the Keynesian sense has solved most of the economic problems that beset the pre-Keynesian world. If there has been a decline of new investment and a consequent growth of unemployment, this means only that still more government-induced production and consumption are required to lead the economy to a fuller use of its productive resources. But these proposals are made without regard to their consequence and without consideration of the real character of the mixed economy.

2

In order to understand the dynamics of the mixed economy, it is necessary to know its working mechanism. The mechanism is provided by government expenditures which counteract the movement from prosperity to depression. The economic role of government seems to divide the whole of the mixed economy into a 'public sector' and a 'private sector'. Actually, of course, it is just one economy in which government intervenes, for it is not government ownership but government control which characterises the mixed economy. There is, of course, in addition, a great and growing amount of direct ownership in the mixed economy, just as there was government ownership in *laissez-faire* capitalism. But no matter how self-supporting, self-liquidating, or even profitable some government undertakings are, government still requires an increasingly larger portion of privately-produced national wealth.

The private sector of the economy, to use these familiar terms, differs from the public sector in that the latter is basically non-profitable, the former, profitable. The private sector expands of its own accord, the public sector largely at the expense of the private sector. As long as the growth of the private sector is faster than that of the public sector, the growth of the latter merely reflects the general growth of the economy. It is quite otherwise when the public sector develops faster than the private sector.

Generally, government does not produce for the market. It merely mobilises private savings in order to utilise privately-owned means of production which, in turn, employ labour that would otherwise be idle. The greater national product brought forth in this manner will impair the profitability of private capital, not of particular capitals, to be sure, but in general. It is private production which must yield the taxes necessary to cover government-created 'demand' and to finance its borrowings.

It can be argued, of course, that apart from war, government increases its economic activity only because private production begins to slacken and that, therefore, its profitability remains unaffected since business would not be any better without government intervention. This may well be so, but nonetheless, taxes and the servicing of the national debt must come out of the private sector of the economy and, to that extent, deprive this sector of part of its present and future income. Only if the private sector income rises proportionally faster than the national debt and tax burden, and only if it owes this rise to the 'pump-priming' activities of government, can it be said that government-induced production serves private capital as well.

As far as Keynes was concerned, government intervention in the economy could range from manipulated interest rates to the usurpation of entrepreneurial functions by government. To compete directly with private capital for the available market demand would, however, lead to the gradual displacement of private enterprise by state enterprise and this it cannot be expected to do in a society in which government represents the free enterprise system. Lowering interest rates may, or may not, foster capital investment but this has proven insufficient in periods of stagnation. Increasing taxes for expenditures above the given market demand merely distributes the available income and does not guarantee an increase of employment and production. It may well have the opposite effect, even if income distribution by way of taxes should increase the propensity to consume. While consumption may thus be increased, the inducement to invest may be still further weakened.

Quite generally, then, capitalists propose exactly the opposite procedure – a reduction of taxes to increase the inducement to invest. If their wishes are granted their incomes will be larger, but even this may lead not to a faster rate of capital formation but merely to a greater mass of idle capital. There is no certainty that tax policies, affecting either the propensity to consume or the inducement to invest, will actually lead to an increase of national production and full employment. There is the possibility, however, that employment and production will increase when the government pays out more than it receives by way of taxes, that is, through deficit financing.

Money may be saved instead of being invested or consumed. A low rate of investment may indicate the existence of such savings, a condition Keynes called 'liquidity preference'. The government can borrow these savings and increase its expenditures and, as a result, step up national production and consumption. This process yields profits to some capitalists and interest to others; its financial manifestation is to be found in the national debt and in an increasing ratio of taxes to national product.

Not only government deficit financing but a large part of private production is based on credit, on the expectation, that is, that further economic growth will be profitable enough to take care of the indebtedness. Corporate debts are not liquidated in the aggregate but are refunded with new bond issues that take the place of those coming due. Credit being continuous, expansion can also be continuous. Government debts are handled in the same fashion. Whatever it borrows and spends, the government need not directly worry about repayments, for it can again borrow an equal or greater amount.

Private expansion by way of credits is bound to an expected profitability and the expected profitability, to the actual profitability of capital. It is the latter which encourages or discourages private credit expansion. A static, or declining, rate of capital formation implies a contraction of the private credit structure. This can be compensated through government borrowings. In this way the government avails itself of privately-owned productive resources. This 'transfer' of economic control stimulates a 'demand' of a specific kind, namely, a nonmarket demand for public undertakings above those that 'normally' fall under the category of government expenditures. The same principle which made the actual war economy a full-employment economy also increases economic activity in the mixed economy, or rather, the former distinction between wartime and peacetime production has largely disappeared and the mixed economy operates, though to a lesser extent, as if it were a permanent war economy. In this way, and until recently, the mixed economy has been sufficiently 'stabilised' to sidetrack such depressions as those that occurred in the period between the two world wars.

3

A period of economic expansion need not be inflationary, even though the money supply increases with the rising debt, because productivity may increase sufficiently to equate the social supply and demand. In any case, it is not the quantity of money and the effect of the credit mechanism upon the quantity of money which determines price relations and the state of production. Rather, it is the other way around; the state of social production determines its profitability and, therewith, price and money relations. An excessive monetary growth by way of credit expansion and deficit financing may, however, lead to inflation, just as credit contraction and too little money tends to be deflationary. There must be the 'right' quantity of money to avoid both excessive inflation and excessive deflation and, according to Keynes, it is the government's function to arrange for this 'right quantity'. Fiscal policies toward this end are, of course, also monetary policies as they merely allocate the 'right quantity' of money in the direction most conducive to economic stability and growth.

The Keynesians see the economy as a money economy and tend to forget that it is a money-making economy. In their views money appears as a mere instrument of manipulation for turning insufficient into sufficient social production. In the prevailing society, however, money is the beginning and the end of production; a given quantity of money, or capital, must be turned via the production process into a greater quantity. Capitalist production and capital accumulation are synonymous.

As in early capitalism, so in the mixed economy, capital is not accumulated to increase production, but production is increased to accumulate capital. National production can be increased through the accumulation of private and public debts, but the accumulation of debts is not the accumulation of capital. It is for this reason that the private credit structure contracts as soon as the expansion of production is not an accumulation of capital. It is only the accumulation of public debts which can enlarge social production where and when it fails to increase of its own accord, i.e. through capital formation determined by the market.

The increase of social demand through government purchases with borrowed money has been an inflationary process. Usually, inflation is defined as a situation wherein the national money income is rising faster than the national real income, i.e. where there is too much money in relation to the available goods. If it were true that government financing increases production generally, as its advocates claim, this rising production should close the gap between money income and real income and, thus, end the initial inflationary pressure. But inflation, however creeping, is continuous. Apparently, there is always too much money in relation to available supplies. In fact, however, there is an abundance of goods and not enough purchasing power. The inflation is, thus, not explainable as a situation in which too much money chases an insufficient quantity of goods. It is rather a mechanism which curtails consumption regardless of the supply so as to mitigate the loss of profitability caused by government-induced production.

4

Economists are not in the habit of distinguishing between government-induced production and private capital formation, between government-created demand and market demand. They think of capital formation as a mere addition of tools to turn out more products no matter what these products may be. So long as total national production in terms of money is growing and unemployment is held in check they are satisfied. Only when stagnation displaces expansion do they start looking for more 'permanent' sources of demand.

What could these sources be? Private capital formation by way of the production of marketable goods finds its observable limits in a diminishing market demand. In order not to reduce the marketability of privately produced commodities still further, government-induced production must be channelled into nonmarket fields – public works, armaments, superfluities, and waste. For the same reason, and contrary to Keynes's suggestions, production cannot be increased by way of income distribution that favours the poor.

Although it is true that the economy's actual, or potential, productive capacity would allow for a production of 'abundance', it remains, as regards its profit requirements, a 'scarcity economy'. Because the production of commodities is merely a necessary mechanism for the production of profits and the augmentation of capital, the system's success or failure cannot be measured by the abundance or shortages of commodities but only by the rate of profit and accumulation. Despite a great amount of unsalable surplus production, this system must first raise the profitability of capital before it can enlarge social consuming power through higher wages and greater social welfare.

Wages are 'costs of production' and, if increased without a corresponding larger increase of labour productivity, will reduce the profitability of capital. Wages do rise under capitalism, but only under conditions of rapid capital accumulation. Capital formation represents the excess of production over what society consumes. It may, and generally does, lead to increased consumption, but consumption itself cannot lead to capital formation.

Each capital entity, whether large or small, must try to keep its production costs at a minimum in order to reach the profit maximum. Extra profits through monopolisation and price manipulation increase competition between the less privileged capital entities and transfer profits from the weaker to the stronger enterprises. Although a partial escape from competition frees some enterprises from a steady and pressing concern with production costs, it magnifies this concern for other enterprises. In the long run, of course, the resulting decrease of profitability of the more competitive enterprises will also decrease the amount of profits that can be transferred to the less competitive capitals. Although, actually, the whole process is played out in the market sphere, it has its source, and finds its limits, in the sphere of production.

As long as competition prevails it will centre on the costs of production and will, thus, determine wages to the extent that they cannot be larger than is compatible with an enterprise's profitability. To the extent that greater profitability is reached through profit transfers via the marketing and price mechanism, higher wages in some enterprises are based on correspondingly lower wages in others. Just as the total social profit cannot be increased by the 'inequality' of profit distribution, so total wages at any one time remain what they are no matter how they may be distributed among different labouring groups.

Government determination of wages presupposes government determination of profits and vice versa, and each is equally impossible within the market economy whether mixed or not. The demand for a higher propensity to consume by way of higher wages amounts to a request for ending the market economy and, if taken seriously, would require centralised control of the whole of the economy and a planned determination of its production, consumption, and expansion. Short of this, the propensity to consume will vary with the ability to accumulate capital. It is for this reason that government-manipulated wage increases are not among the various 'built-in stabilisers' of the mixed economy, and that it is always the lowest wage which sets the standard for government minimum wage legislation.

Increasing the propensity to consume through the redistribution of income in favour of the poorer classes should show up in income statistics. Where it does, it does so only through 'interpretation', not as an undisputable fact. Recent studies of income distribution have revealed that, although wages have increased, the distribution of national income among the different classes has hardly changed. There have been shifts within the high-income brackets and some of these shifts undoubtedly reflect the expansion of the economy's public sector at the expense of the private sector. Despite these shifts, however, and with regard to total social production – private and public – the gap between production and consumption gets wider, not narrower. Because an increasing part of social production is of a nonprofitable nature, the decline of private capital production appears as an apparent redistribution of income without increasing the propensity to consume, least of all by way of higher wages.

5

It is not by increasing the propensity to consume, in the proper sense of the term, that the mixed economy solves the problem of insufficient effective demand. Yet, it does increase employment and production by way of 'consumption'; but this 'consumption' takes on the form of public works and the production of waste, predominantly in the form of armaments. As far as private capital 'as a whole' is concerned, the government-induced part of total production falls out of the market system and thus out of the private accumulation process. It falls in the sphere of consumption where it is irretrievably lost.

This reverses the traditional procedure of capital formation. Instead of expanding capital at the expense of consumption through 'savings', it expands production by expanding government expenditures that lie in the sphere of consumption. Nonetheless, recent history has demonstrated that it is possible to have a 'prosperous' development under conditions of relatively shrinking markets and government-induced production because of the high level of productivity. When kept within definite bounds relative to the total profitability of the national economy, government-induced production may just compensate for the declining market demand without seriously impairing either the profitability of capital or the propensity to consume. The costs of government-induced production may be tolerable because they are distributed over the whole of society, and over a long period of time, by way of inflation and deficit financing. However, if too much of social production is consumed in whatever form, there is not only a smaller supply of capital for investment purposes but also a lower rate of profit for the existing capital and, consequently, a diminishing incentive to invest. When the increase in government-induced production is enough to reduce private capital formation absolutely, the gain in production by way of this type of production will once more be lost through the loss of production via private capital expansion. A further increase in government-induced production would then be possible only at the expense of consumption in that term's true sense.

This process may be understood by analogy with the war economy in which the increasing amount of waste production is realised by way of consumption restrictions as well as at the expense of new capital investments. Eventually, however, it is only at the expense of consumption, for the continuation and enlargement of waste production requires the replacement and extension of the productive apparatus. Under actual war conditions waste production increases at an ever-faster rate, while waste production in anticipation of war, or as a means to full employment, can be kept under control. Nonetheless, a steady, if slow, increase of waste production in the mixed economy requires the maintenance of a certain rate of capital formation, and the need for both this definite rate of capital formation and the necessary amount of waste production will eventually have to be secured at the expense of consumption.

6

What is here called waste production, i.e. that amount of social production carried on to compensate for the relative stagnation of private capital production, appears to the capitalists as an unavoidable, if even at times regrettable, necessity. It appears as necessary not only to those whose profits, or livelihood, depend on it, but quite generally. Unable, or at any rate unwilling, to admit to any inherent contradictions in the prevailing mode of production, or to its long-run incompatibility with social progress, economic difficulties are laid at the door of external enemies who provide the rationale for the growing waste production.

Indeed, a continuous capital accumulation appears theoretically conceivable as long as the growing productivity of labour provides the profits necessary to this end. There will be a continuous displacement of labour by machinery relative to growing capital, but this does not exclude an absolutely growing labour force. Likewise, the increase of exploitation can be accompanied by a continuous betterment of living conditions. However, profits must be not only produced but also realised by way of sales. The expansion of capital must be the expansion of the capitalist market.

Taking the market into consideration, a given mass of capital may be simultaneously too large and too small, that is, it may be too large with regard to the realisation of profits by way of sales and, at the same time, too small to be able to enlarge the market by way of an enhanced productivity. The American economy, for instance, produced in 1962 about twenty per cent below its capacity, and this in spite of the great amount of government-induced production. It could increase production by almost one-fifth of the present national product without additional capital equipment and without exhausting the labour supply. Yet, it could not profitably sell the increased output, and it could not give it away, either, without cutting down on sales that are still profitable. In view of the present market, the production of the American economy is obviously too large; nor does there seem to be any way of realising profits from a still larger production.

Nevertheless, to all bourgeois economists existing capital appears too small; all of them clamour for a faster rate of capital formation. This would, of course, increase production and require correspondingly larger markets, although even the existing capital equipment is not fully utilised. For the 'radical' Keynesians this presents no problem. In their reasoning, extra market demand can be created at will through additional government spending and a further distribution of income to stimulate the propensity to consume. But governments of mixed economies represent the interests of private capital. Economic expansion by way of deficit spending is a slow form of profit expropriation and is resorted to because governments do not want to expropriate capital. Too much deficit financing, however, is a slow form of capital expropriation and it is only the force of circumstances, not the ideas of the Keynesians, which will induce governments to increase production by a continuous increase of the national debt.

Aside from all theory, capitalists, too, see a larger capital as a solution to economic problems. Only under conditions of rapid capital formation will social demand be large enough to employ all, or nearly all, productive resources. Under *laissez-faire* conditions, the overproduction of capital, and the overproduction of commodities as its market expression, was always overcome, after a period of depression, by an enhanced capital accumulation. Profits which could not be realised on a smaller scale of production could be realised on a larger scale of production. Whereas the smaller capital had been unprofitable, the larger capital was once again profitable. The reason for this was to be found in the structural changes which capital underwent during the depression period. A larger scale of production for relatively fewer enterprises and a more favourable relationship between wages and profits restored a previously lost 'balance' between capital accumulation and its profitability.

Unused capacity is held to be one more reason for achieving a larger capital. The unused equipment is considered 'obsolete' because it is not competitive and, therefore, not profitable. In fact, a full use of capacity would be less profitable than its partial use, not only because there is no corresponding demand for a larger production but because many firms and corporations are competitive (nationally as well as internationally) only in so far as they operate with, and limit themselves to, the most up-to-date technical equipment and the lowest labour costs. In order to increase their markets, they must become still more competitive, i.e. increase the 'obsolescence' of their capital equipment by an enhanced capital formation.

A larger capital represents a more efficient productive apparatus able to outproduce less efficient capitals, thus capturing their markets as well as enlarging the market generally. Designed and built up, in the first place, with a view towards an expanding world market, the productive apparatus of capitalistically-advanced countries exceeds the scope of their national markets. The combined production of the industrial nations exceeds the scope of the world market, unless a general, rapid capital formation expands the world market as fast as international production. While this is not impossible, it is seldom the case. Some nations accumulate faster, or suffer more severe depressions, than others. The resulting changes in economic power relations are also experienced as shifts in political power relations, and national economic competition turns into imperialistic competition and war.

Under nineteenth-century conditions it was easier to overcome a temporary over-accumulation of capital by means of depressions, which more or less affected capital on an international scale. At the turn of the century, it was no longer possible to change the international capital structure by way of depression and to reach, thereby, a new basis for the resumption of the accumulation process. What was still possible nationally was no longer effective internationally because, more than before, economic competition was now supplemented with political-military competition. The international concentration of capital, necessary for the resumption of the capital accumulation process, was no longer an 'automatic' result of economic crisis but could only be brought about directly, through government 'interventions' by way of war.

The resumption of the accumulation process in the wake of a 'strictly' economic crisis increased the general scale of production. War, too, resulted in increased economic activity. In either case, capital emerged more concentrated and centralised both in spite of and because of the accomplished destruction of capital. Despite the losses of some nations, the gains of others were large enough to initiate an apparently new period of general capital expansion, soon to exceed, in terms of world production, pre-war levels of production. In its effect, then, war production was not really waste production but a medium for the resumption of the capital formation process. In this sense, waste production was not only a subsidy to armaments producers but a precondition for the profitability of postwar capitalism. This is an additional reason why, generally, capitalists object to useful public works and welfare spending but not to an increase in 'defence' expenditures. Aside from ideological considerations, experience shows that economic difficulties can be resolved by force, or that the retainment of economic privileges may require military intervention.

These notions are no doubt insane in view of the destructiveness of atomic warfare. It is, however, impossible to proceed rationally in an irrational society. The recognition that war can no longer solve the problems that beset the capitalist world does not prevent a form of behaviour which may lead to war. No capitalist desired the losses of depression, yet the relentless competition for capital nonetheless led into crisis and depression; in other words, it was 'normal' behaviour which caused the 'abnormality' of the crisis. It is not different with regard to war. The relentless drive for political and economic dominance, either to gain or to retain it, is the outcome and sum total of all the asocial behaviour that comprises social life under capitalism.

The recognition that war will be suicide does not affect the drift towards war, and those who make political decisions are no less trapped in this cul-de-sac than the emasculated and indifferent masses. Simply by making the 'right' decisions, as determined by the specific needs of their nations and the security of their social structures, they may destroy themselves and a large part of the world. They may realise the 'obsolescence' of war, yet they cannot help preparing for it because a disarmed capitalism would soon cease to exist. They prepare for war not only because the production of waste provides some kind of economic stability, but even more so because of an unspoken suspicion, if not awareness, that nothing really guarantees the future of capitalism except terrorisation of the world. Because of the enormity of nuclear war, the hope is often expressed that such a war will be averted, although it is granted that it may break out 'accidentally'. Without decisive social changes, however, it will be the avoidance of war which will be the 'accident' rather than its occurrence.

7

The Second World War failed to provide the impetus for a private capital expansion, determined by the market, on a scale sufficient to diminish government-induced demand. Any significant decrease of government spending in the postwar world led to economic contractions which could be altered only through the resumption of large-scale government spending. The best that could be expected was the stabilisation of the relationship between private production and government spending as it emerged in the postwar world. But even this required a definite rate of economic growth in order to keep the economy competitive and to prevent the rise of unemployment. While governments tried to foster capital formation, their lack of success in this respect required an increase in government-induced production which put new obstacles in the way of private capital expansion. At times both policies were tried – the improvement of capitalist earnings by way of tax reductions and the increase of waste production through more deficit financing. But as the deficit must be financed out of private production, this merely amounts to giving with the one hand what the other takes away, even though the process is thereby stretched out over a longer period of time.

How long a time? This is an unanswerable question and just because it cannot be answered the argument in favour of larger government deficits appears convincing. Perhaps, there will come a time, allowing for private capital formation rapid and large enough to catch up with the rising national debt and keep it within manageable proportions. Perhaps not, but even this can be justified on the principle: 'after us, the deluge'.

How much can a government tax and borrow? Obviously not the whole of the national product. Perhaps fifty per cent? This would come close to wartime conditions during which the American Government purchased roughly half of the national product. Under these conditions, however, the rate of investment was 2.9 percent of gross national product – a rate below that of the depression years, with the sole exception of 1932, when the rate dropped to 1.5 percent. A war economy, however, if indefinitely continued, will destroy the capitalist system. An increase of waste production up to fifty percent in the peacetime mixed economy would be equivalent to the conditions of the war economy, except that waste products deteriorate slowly instead of being destroyed outright. However, actual waste production in the United States, i.e. the military budget, comprises roughly ten percent of gross national product, while total government expenditures account for about one-fourth of gross national product. There is still considerable leeway before the conditions of the peacetime economy approach those of the wartime economy.

Private capital can exist and even flourish despite a high ratio of government spending to national product. There is, of course, an absolute ceiling where taxation will reduce rather than increase social production via the public sector. But what this ceiling is precisely, or when it will be reached, is not predictable. The ratio of taxes to national income in the mixed economies varies between one-fourth and one-third. England has the highest and the United States the lowest ratio. Government intervention in the West European nations, however, did not imply the growth of waste production but the revival of recapitalisation of the market economy. Governments arranged for compulsory, or near-compulsory, institutional savings, and for the retention of a large share of corporate profits for reinvestment purposes. Expansion was achieved by way of deficit financing and inflation.

This forced recapitalisation of Western Europe was not the result of the application of the 'new economics'; rather, the 'application' worked in this particular way because of the conditions in which Europe found itself after the war. The enormous destruction of capital, both in value and in physical terms, and the obsolescence of a large part of the surviving productive apparatus allowed for, and demanded, a rapid capital formation to avoid a total collapse of the private property system. Both capital and labour accepted the demands of government to work not for more consumption but for capital accumulation. And, as in times past, more consumption became a by-product of the accelerated expansion process.

The same 'economics' did not have similar results in the United States because there was no destruction of capital in either value or physical terms. To maintain the greatly augmented production after the war, and to enlarge it, required a far greater control of the world economy than was actually achievable. Such control could not be realised at the expense of European capitalism; on the contrary, it required Europe's recovery. Private property capitalism simply cannot become a world economy controlled from a particular centre, such as the United States. Just as in each capitalist nation, the capital concentration process cannot complete itself without destroying the competitive market economy, so, internationally, capitalism cannot integrate under the dominance of a particular nation. Economic integration of the world economy presupposes political integration, and this is an impossibility because of the competitive nature of capital production in a market economy. What was possible after the war was a return to pre-war conditions modified by the political changes resulting from the war, that is, the restoration of a truncated European economy to a world market made smaller by the further spread of autarchism in various nations, and the emergence of a competitive 'second' world market through the consolidation of the Eastern power bloc.

Under certain conditions, then, a mixed economy may expand its market demand and private capital formation in spite of a high ratio of taxes to national income, whereas another mixed economy, under different conditions, may not be able to increase the market demand and private capital formation despite a lower ratio of taxes to national product. Western Europe's 'prosperous' rate of capital formation has its source in conditions resulting from the Second World War. With the ending of the special influences due to these conditions, Western Europe, like the United States, will most probably have to resort to more waste production to avoid a new economic decline.

8

Whatever the ratio of taxes to national income, government-induced production comes up against the limitations of profitable market production. So long as the 'private sector' dominates, there is no way of indulging in production free of profit considerations except via the profit production of private capital. The limits of private profit production are, finally, also the limits of government-induced material production. Where private capital dominates, state intervention in the economy cannot go beyond the point where it would seriously threaten private capital production. If the economy cannot 'prosper' at this point it will not 'prosper'. To change this situation through farther-reaching interventions would now require the existence of governments able and willing to destroy the social dominance of private capital and to proceed from government control to government ownership.

Because government control in the mixed economy subordinates itself to existing property relations, it serves, at this stage of the game, the interests of big business. What redistribution of income there is consists, to a large extent, of a shifting of tax money from non-subsidised to subsidised sections of the economy. It aids the concentration of capital through the subsidisation of big business, the main supplier of government-created demand.

Although production by subsidisation helps to secure the profitability of durable, such as defence, industries, it lowers the profitability of non-subsidised industries. The increase of production lowers the social average rate of profit, derived, as it is, from the profitability of total social capital, and impairs the general ability to increase profitability by way of new investments. The market for durable goods shrinks, so to speak, despite the continued growth of the durable goods producing industries. Moreover, unless subsidised by government, there is no real incentive to invest because of the bleak market outlook. Competition could force expansion just the same, but in a highly concentrated capital structure, price agreements rather than competition appear preferable. In key industries, prices are freed of all market pressures and are pushed up as unused capacity increases, thus forcing price increases upon all dependent industries. Prices rise despite the still-increasing productivity of labour which now fails to operate as of old, namely, as a way to larger markets.

In three different ways, then, big business secures its profitability even under conditions of a low rate of capital formation. First, through the exploitation of its own workers; second, through partaking in the results of exploitation of other capitalists; and finally, through government subsidies which transfer tax money extracted from all layers of society to big business. What profit it appropriates must come from other sectors of the economy, thereby lowering their own ability to expand. Once waste production becomes a permanent and institutionalised factor in social production, a vicious circle begins to operate. By increasing government-induced production, private capital accumulation diminishes; the diminution of private capital formation increases government-induced production; this, in turn, diminishes private capital expansion, and so on.

How to break out of this vicious circle? 'Theoretically', there are two possibilities, both equally impossible in practice. Both have to do with the 'unmixing' of the mixed economy, either by a return to a 'free' market economy such as prevailed in the past, or by ending the market economy as a mixed economy altogether. Unable to return to the conditions of the past and unable to transform itself into a state capitalist system, the mixed economy alternates between stagnation and destruction, between insufficient capital expansion and increased waste production. It is, then, not a manifestation of capitalism's ability to 'reform' itself by realising the golden mean of just the right amount of government control and just the right amount of private initiative for the 'optimum' achievement of 'economic efficiency', but a manifestation of the rather 'permanent' crisis condition in which capitalism has found itself since the beginning of this century.

CHAPTER 8

Henryk Grossman and Crisis Theory

The publication of Henryk Grossman's main work, *The Law of Accumulation and Breakdown of the Capitalist System*,[1] coincided with the beginning of the Great Depression of 1929 and attracted special attention for that reason alone. Besides this, the work was also an important scientific achievement because it restored the marxian theory of accumulation from oblivion to a position of prominence within socialist discussions. The relatively long periods of progressive capitalist development which ended with the world war had influenced the reformist practices of the labour movement as well as its theory and found expression in the doctrine of revisionism. In the revisionist conception, capitalism developed differently than Marx had expected. One could no longer assume that its development would be circumscribed by objective limits. Because an economic breakdown of the system could not be expected, one had to limit oneself to social policy. The use of bourgeois democracy would lead to steady improvement in the condition of the working class and eventually to the establishment of a socialist society.

Although it is possible to combine a reformist practice with a revolutionary ideology, it is utterly impossible to pursue a revolutionary practice with a reformist theory. The radical wing of the socialist movement understood that without an objective need for revolution, there would be no subjective readiness for it either. It wasn't enough to oppose reformism, one had to also deny its success with proof that now as ever the contradictions of the capitalist system would lead to its eventual downfall. If one assumes a limitless expansion of capital accumulation, wrote Rosa Luxemburg, 'socialism ... ceases to be an historical necessity'.[2] She attempted to provide the proof that the domination of capital was beset by self-generated objective limits.

Luxemburg's book, *The Accumulation of Capital*, was rejected by most everyone, either because she presented her ideas as a critique of marxian theory, or because the book's premises contradicted social-democratic ideology. Grossman set himself the task of deducing Luxemburg's conviction of an inevitable end of capitalism from Marx's theory itself, as Luxemburg had only suggested but had not found possible. He proved that Luxemburg was correct in relationship to the reformists, even though her Marx-critique was based on an error.

1 Grossmann 1929.
2 Luxemburg 2015, p. 376.

For Grossman, as for Marx, the difficulties and limits that capitalism experiences can be traced ideologically and practically to its relations of production. For Luxemburg, though, it wasn't the production of profits but their realisation on the market that accounted for the orientation towards crises. Surplus-value could not be fully realised, in her opinion, within the capital- and wage-labour relationships. For that, a non-capitalist world was needed. With the ongoing capitalisation of the world, however, the possibility of an uninterrupted process of capital accumulation also disappeared. This theory explained for Luxemburg the imperialist character of capitalist competition.

According to Marx, the circulation of commodities was inseparable from their production, so that difficulties in the production of capital also appeared as difficulties in the realisation of surplus-value. It was obvious that even without a realisation problem, contradictions within the sphere of production would remain. The tendency towards crises and the historical end of capitalism was already presupposed within the relations of production. It was thanks to Grossman that the debate on accumulation was refocused on relations of production and the marxist understanding of value and surplus-value production.

Bourgeois economics barely bothers with the issue of accumulation, a discussion that is reserved almost exclusively for marxism. The controversy over Luxemburg's accumulation theory not only found new life through Grossman's book, which also included its own interpretation of marxian theory. To a great extent, the debate hinged on questions of marxist methodology and the role and meaning of abstraction, with reference to empirical conditions and developmental tendencies within capitalism. According to Luxemburg, the abstract methodology employed in volumes one and two of *Capital* – the analysis of value and surplus-value in a closed system consisting exclusively of workers and capitalists – was 'only a theoretical premise whose purpose is to facilitate and simplify the inquiry'.[3] This obviously contradicted reality. Although Luxemburg had nothing against such a procedure, she missed in Marx the necessary concretisation of abstract insights, which in her opinion would show that without non-capitalist lands, 'it is impossible for the capitalist class as a whole to rid itself of its excess commodities in order to convert surplus-value into money and thus be able to accumulate capital'.[4]

For Luxemburg, Marx had 'only posed the question of total social capital, but didn't provide the answer'.[5] She based her assertion on an investigation of

---

3 Luxemburg 2015, p. 359.
4 Ibid.
5 Luxemburg 2015, p. 363.

the reproduction schemes in the second volume of Marx's *Capital*, which illustrated the simple and expanded reproduction of capital. In order to demonstrate clearly the division in the economy between means of production and means of consumption, the exchange between the two departments occurs without difficulty and guarantees the required equilibrium necessary for both simple and expanded reproduction. Marx used these schemata in order to show that exchange is determined not only by values but also by use-values. He concluded that the capitalist mode of production engenders 'certain conditions for normal exchange that are peculiar to this mode of production, i.e. conditions for the normal course of reproduction, whether simple or on an expanded scale, which turn into an equal number of conditions for an abnormal course, possibilities of crises, since, on the basis of the spontaneous pattern of this production, this balance is itself an accident'.[6] These schemes do not assume a frictionless accumulation process but instead illustrate the equilibrium conditions necessary for reproduction, which within capitalism occur only accidentally, similar to the determination of value and price, or supply and demand, which also only accidently coincide.

Although Luxemburg later acknowledged that her interpretation of Marx's reproduction schemes was neither accurate nor necessary, that 'on the matter of accumulation, mathematical schemas can prove absolutely nothing',[7] her critics used her arguments about the reproduction schemes to show a crisis-free accumulation of capital. This was particularly true of Otto Bauer, who designed reproduction schemes that supposedly contradicted Luxemburg's interpretation and demonstrated instead a harmonious, limitless accumulation process. It was on this matter that Grossman directed his criticisms, as much against Luxemburg as against Otto Bauer. About the latter, Grossman used Bauer's own assumptions to demonstrate that the process of accumulation would lead to an economic breakdown, if not within the timespan used by Bauer, then in an expanded length of time. This did not mean that a collapse of the capitalist system could be modelled schematically, only that Bauer's 'proof' of a limitless expansion actually proved just the opposite.

That Grossman began with Luxemburg's discussion of Marx's reproduction schemes overshadowed his own contribution to the marxian theory of accumulation, which was based on conditions of neither equilibrium nor disequilibrium regarding the exchanges between economic spheres, but on the tendency of the rate of profit to decline in response to the growth in the organic composition of capital during the course of accumulation. This was a

---

6 Marx 1981, p. 571.
7 Luxemburg 2015, p. 367.

logical consequence of marxian value theory as applied to the process of accumulation, from which the dual character of commodities as exchange-value and use-value evolved in consequence of the increased productivity of labour. Enhanced productivity, growth in the organic composition of capital, the tendency of the rate of profit to decline, and the accumulation process were for Marx simply aspects of one and the same process, which when viewed theoretically, were independent of the conditions of exchange between the two major economic departments, which in any case must first be understood under the concept of total capital.

In all probability, it was the intensive occupation with the reproduction schemes that prompted Grossman to take a new look at issues regarding Marx's methodology. Marx's writings and letters indicate several different plans for *Capital*. In particular, he abandoned the original plan to write six separate volumes that would each address a distinct problematic aspect of the capitalist economy in favour of a more general and abstract presentation that finally resulted in the three volumes of *Capital* plus the additional *Theories of Surplus Value*. Grossman became convinced that 'a necessary internal connection exists between the change in the plan for Marx's work and the methodological construction of the reproduction schema'.[8]

Grossman saw the reproduction schemes as a means to introduce the circulation of material goods into the designs for *Capital*. This assumption makes little sense. One could just as easily say that the reproduction schemes more likely derive from the methodology employed previously by Marx's *Outlines of a Critique of Political Economy*.[9] The debate among marxists[10] over the issue of whether or not Marx had fundamentally altered his original plans or simply had not completed them, has little meaning, if only because one can say with Luxemburg that *Capital* represents a 'torso' for an unfinished work that needs to be extended. Grossman intended among other things to reject this view and show that the 'the material left to us by Marx is essentially finished, apart from the details of exposition' and 'constitutes a finished, i.e. complete, system'.[11]

In any case, it is seemingly irrelevant whatever Marx intended; what can be discussed are the published manuscripts and the methods of representation used within them. Marx's method of isolating specific variables as a means to construct a model that highlights solely capitalism's essential components and the laws that govern them is independent of the reproduction schemes,

---

8   Grossman 2013, p. 144.
9   Marx 1973.
10 Morf 1951.
11 Grossman 2013, p. 162.

itself an expression of the methodology. It is obvious that Marx elaborated this methodology in the course of his investigations and that it had more important applications in his later than in his earlier works. But already in the *Grundrisse*, Marx relied on certain abstractions in order to capture the laws governing the capitalist mode of production, and here too he came to the same findings regarding capitalism's laws of motion that are described in *Capital*.

According to Grossman, the reproduction schemes were a necessary moment in Marx's method of simplification, since the exchange of commodities requires at least two separate producers. The reproduction schemes divide total capital into two groups. With Marx, nonetheless, capitalism's laws of motion refer to capital in general, even though total capital does not actually exist in reality. For Marx, the idea of total capital, or capital in general, is indeed an abstraction, but not an arbitrary one. It's clear that all the capitals that exist at any one time together comprise the total capital, even though their total extent is not measurable, and what is true for each individual capital is especially true for capital in general, namely the production of surplus-value.

According to Marx, the fall in the profit rate is an expression of the declining relationship between surplus-value and the mass of total capital, regardless of how it is divided among the individual capitals or even if there were only two productive departments in consideration. That does not imply that Marx extended the concept of total capital to the reproduction schemes simply in order to show how exchange functions, since this needs no justification. The reproduction schemes refer to the circulation process of an expanding capital that is based on the production of surplus-value. The expanded reproduction of total capital is indeed a process of circulation, both for each individual capital and for capital taken as a whole. Whatever difficulties are specific to the circulation process are already presupposed in the basic relationship between wage-labour and capital and between capital in general and wage-labour in general. These set limits on the reproduction process as a process of the circulation of capital.

Value theory is based on the concept of total capital, since on this level value and price are identical. However, the total surplus-value is transformed and distributed through the competitive process into prices of production and eventually into market prices. The total surplus-value determines the rate of profit and the rate of accumulation for the total capital. The organic composition of total capital, like that of the individual capitals, is altered during the process of accumulation. That is, constant capital grows faster than variable and the rate of profit falls, and even though it is calculated on total capital, it is only produced by the variable portion. This is not the case, however, when the exploitation of labour power increases faster that the organic composition of capital. According to Marx, however, this is not sustainable in the long term.

The intensified exploitation is limited by an ever-declining number of employees and by absolute limits both socially and naturally relative to the expanding capital.

In this sense, the marxian theory of accumulation is not dependent on the reproduction schemes. The schemes simply show that an exchange of value is not possible. The circulation process for total capital is portrayed in terms of prices of production, a result of the competitive process and the market mechanism. Because it is not possible to ascertain values from prices, or the opposite, prices from values, the reproduction schemes can only be understood with the implausible assumption of equal values, which nonetheless do not have the same theoretical justification as does the abstract concept of total capital. Even though total prices are identical with total values for total capital, in exchange prices always deviate from values. The reproduction schemes illustrate the circulation process of total capital through the false assumption of value exchange, simply as a means to illustrate anything at all. The distinct entities within the schemes do not illustrate the possibility of reproduction, but instead are arbitrarily constructed in order to show a particular process. Neither the possibility nor impossibility of a harmonious reproduction process for total capital has been proven. All that is shown is that exchange must be implemented in specific proportions.

Independently of whether one views, along with Grossman, the reproduction schemes as a necessary aspect or even the starting point for a marxian methodology, or whether the marxist interpretation of the accumulation process is independent of the reproduction schemes, Grossman's debate with Luxemburg and her followers had useful results. As in his major work, the issue of capital accumulation was newly addressed, such that his focus on the reproduction schemes clarified the controversial issue of the value-price transformation problem.[12] The ostensible contradiction between the first and third volumes of *Capital* discovered by Böhm-Bawerk,[13] namely, between an analysis conducted on the basis of values and the reality of an economy governed by prices, had also prompted a re-examination within marxian circles that was only tentatively refuted.[14] This confusion mirrored the controversy engendered by Luxemburg's reproduction schemes and consequently offered Grossman an opportunity to clarify these issues.

Marx's model of capitalist accumulation abstracts from many aspects of reality in order to clarify the underlying logic of that system. For one, it assumes

---

12   Grossman 2016; also Grossmann 1971.
13   Böhm-Bawerk 2011.
14   Hilferding 2011.

an equivalence of values based on labour-time. It presupposes a system that contains only workers and capitalists. This view of value and surplus-value is not only a 'simplified first level' of analysis, but a necessary abstraction in order to comprehend concrete conditions. In this sense, value theory was for Marx the 'science' of political economy. It is more than a preliminary assumption, since it maintains its justification even after those aspects of concrete reality that were at first ignored are incorporated into the analysis. The abstract law of value dominates reality, even though the latter seems to deviate from the law of value. The law of value is not only a tool of investigation but also a part of reality itself, which nonetheless can only be uncovered conceptually rather than be discovered empirically. There is no need to correct it after the fact with reality. It is a part of reality, whose dynamic it determines.

The law of value for Marx is not only a scientific method but also a knowledge of actual connections which only seemingly contradict reality. Even though the law of value also underpinned capitalist development for Grossman, his interpretation of Marx's method also led to misunderstandings. For Roman Rosdolsky, for example, the assumption that Marx altered his plans for *Capital* is wrong because Marx's method was developed on the basis of the dialectical methodology found in Hegelian philosophy.[15] Rosdolsky agreed with Lenin and Georg Lukács 'that a whole series of categories of central importance and in constant use stem directly from Hegel's Logic'.[16] It goes without saying, which Grossman would not object to, that Marx viewed social development as a dialectical process, which derived not just from capitalist development but from social development in general. The dialectical stance does not absolve the need to work with the specific, historically given categories which in capitalism appear as economic categories. The production of value and surplus-value applies only to capitalism, and the dialectic of its development can only be expressed through categories which are specific to it.

Not only for Rosdolsky, but also for Grossman, Marx's abstract view of value is not only a precondition for knowledge of the real world, but it also encompasses the entire secret of capitalist development and its unavoidable end. The value perspective, which leaves out of consideration actual categories such as competition, prices, credit, foreign trade, and other forms in which surplus-value is divided – such as profit, interest, and rent – reveals by itself the general law of capital accumulation. This law, however, only manifests itself by means of the competitive process in a world that knows nothing, nor even wants to

---

15   Rosdolsky 1977.
16   Lukács 1971, p. xliv.

know, of either value or surplus-value, and which provides no insight into its actual developmental tendencies. It can also be shown that the actual categories of the capitalist economy have no ability to alter the law of value, that is, the law of value cannot be set aside by apparent contradictions that emanate from the market-place. The third volume of *Capital* is dedicated to this demonstration and, by means of the law of value, makes clear the inner connections between the essence of capitalism and its forms of appearance.

Because Grossman's procedure of successive approximations and Rosdolsky's dialectic both lead to the same result, the methodological differences between them cannot be very great. In both, abstraction leads towards the concrete, the totality dominates its parts, there is a difference between essence and appearance, and the system encounters objective limits. More important are the misunderstandings which resulted from Grossman's criticism of Otto Bauer's reproduction tables, since they reveal the possibility of an automatic breakdown of the capitalist economy. This charge is not entirely unjustified, because Grossman seemed to consider his criticism as an indirect proof of his own breakdown theory, or in any case, attached even more importance to the discussion about the reproduction tables than they seemed to deserve. However that may be, Grossman agreed entirely with Marx regarding accumulation, and consequently, was unsympathetic to the issues that had preoccupied Luxemburg and her critics.

Under the simplifying conventions used by Marx, to view the theory of accumulation as a theory of breakdown, follows logically from the application of the law of value to the process of accumulation. In reality, the tendency toward breakdown is suspended due to counter-tendencies. Crisis-prone development as deduced in theory finds actual expression in the crisis cycle. With the accumulation of capital and changes in its organic composition, the rate of profit declines. At the same time, the rate of surplus-value grows, so that a larger capital with a smaller profit rate produces as much profit or even more as previously with a smaller capital and higher rate of profit. As long as capital grows faster than the rate of profit falls, the fall is only latent. In order to continue, the surplus-value must grow alongside the accelerating rate of accumulation. Should the surplus-value be insufficient for further accumulation, a crisis results, since production without accumulation – or even with the same rate of accumulation – is no longer a capitalistic production.

The fall in the rate of profit accompanies the accumulation process, just as the latter is the fortunate outcome of a falling rate of profit that is countered by the growth of the surplus-value. The declining rate of profit relates to total capital and total surplus-value, and it remains hidden from the individual capital entities. It mirrors the larger social context in which the exchange-value of commodities is lessened due to the growing productivity of labour. Just as this decline is offset by a larger mass of produced goods, so too the increase in surplus-value compensates for the fall in the rate of profit, and only then, when the production of surplus-value nullifies the fall in the profit rate. The amount of surplus-value for such purposes remains unknown, as is true for total capital also. Whether or not it will be sufficient for the continuation of the accumulation process only becomes apparent in the market-place. If a discrepancy emerges between the amount of available surplus-value and the amount needed to continue the accumulation process, it will appear as an overproduction of commodities and a problem of realisation, since the full realisation of profit requires a sufficiently expansive accumulation process.

Marx pointed out the counter-tendencies to the falling rate of profit, but at the same time he also demonstrated that like capitalism itself, these counter-tendencies were historically determined and limited. If social development is not to come to an end with capitalism, it will be due to its class antagonisms. The peculiar class contradictions that are specific to capitalistic productive relations appear as difficulties in the production of value and surplus-value. Just as all previous social development was based on the forces of production, capitalism depends on their further unfolding, which however is only possible by means of capital accumulation. The development of society's productive power means that more can be produced with less labour. Within capitalism, that means faster growth in constant capital than in variable capital, that is, an ever-smaller number of workers in relationship to an ever-faster growing capital. Because the increase in the surplus-value has absolute limits, since workers can neither labour non-stop nor for nothing, the relative decline in the number of workers must lead to a decline in surplus-labour and consequently end in a declining rate of profit that can no longer be counteracted through an increase in surplus-value.

In this sense, there exists for Marx, as for Grossman, a breakdown tendency within capitalism, which nonetheless does not imply that a breakdown occurs 'automatically', or that a timepoint is predictable. What can be said is that on the basis of capitalism's developmental tendencies, the accumulation process is beset with crises, in which every major crisis offers an opportunity to transform the class struggle within society into a struggle for an alternative form of society. Without probing this issue of crises further or examining the mechanism through which a crisis can lead to a new period of prosperity – since this is amply described by Grossman, it can be stressed that the criticism directed against Grossman of an overly schematic and mechanistic interpretation of Marx's theory of accumulation is not pertinent. At best, it is directed against his style of presentation and cannot be carried over to the content. It is clear that one cannot explain everything all at once, and what is missing in a particular piece of work can be found in another. In Grossman's view, 'no economic system, no matter how weakened, collapses by itself in automatic fashion. It must be overthrown'.[17] But that is a matter of the class struggle, not of economic theory, which can merely make known the objective limits under which the class struggle unfolds and which determine its course.

The controversy over accumulation was simply a further expression of the long-established divide within the marxist camp between social reform and revolution. Those who had given up hope for a proletarian revolution and who also detected no need for one proceeded in a new-found conviction that capitalism could be transformed piece-by-piece into a system that served the entire society. Difficulties in the accumulation process were of interest only insofar as they reinforced assumptions regarding their approach to reformist politics. The revolutionaries tended to overestimate economic difficulties in order to lend a sense of objectivity to revolutionary solutions. The alleged 'fatalistic' conviction of an 'unavoidable collapse' of the system did not prevent revolutionary activity, but instead spurred it on. What can also be said is that these different interpretations of Marx's theory of accumulation resulted not only from different class interests but also from different aspects of the class struggle itself.

In contrast to the majority of his work which was focused primarily on theoretical issues pertinent to the socialist movement, Henryk Grossman's 'Marx, Classical Political Economy, and the Problems of Dynamics' is a thorough-going discussion of bourgeois economics. The essay, written to coincide with the seventieth anniversary of Volume 1 of Marx's *Capital*, first appeared in 1940 in a limited edition and did not attract much attention. Grossman turned his attention in this piece against the often repeated but nonetheless false charge that Marx had been a disciple of classical economics. Actually, he was its sharpest opponent and rejected both bourgeois society and the economic theories that it produced. Grossman emphasised that for Marx the categories of bourgeois economics had a fetishistic character that disguised actual social relationships and that only a knowledge of the latter could lead to an understanding of capitalist society and its developmental tendencies.

The labour theory of value began with classical economics. Consequently,

> the existence of the part of the value produced which we now call surplus-value was established long before Marx; what it consists of, i.e. the product of labour, for which the appropriator has paid no equivalent, was also

---

17 Grossman 2017, p. 227.

> formulated with a greater or lesser degree of clarity. But this was as far as it went. Some people – the classical bourgeois economists – investigated primarily the ratio in which the product of labour was distributed between the worker and the proprietor of the means of production. Others – the socialists – found this division unjust and sought to remove the injustice by utopian means. Both remained captive of the economic categories as they had found them ... Then Marx appeared. And he stood in direct opposition to all his predecessors. Where they had seen a solution, he only saw a problem.[18]

The classical economists indeed derived the various forms of value – such as money, prices, wages, interest, and rent – from labouring activity. At the same time, values were mystified, because labour is performed in all social systems, such that one can conclude they all must be based on values. Actually, values have nothing to do with labour, but with labour under capitalistic relations of production. It is these social relationships which transform labour into value and cloth social categories as economic ones, which leads to the obfuscation of the real connections.

Even in its mystified form, the labour theory of value was untenable for the bourgeoisie. Classical political economy, Marx wrote,

> belongs to a period in which the class struggle was as yet undeveloped. Its last great representative, Ricardo, ultimately (and consciously) made the antagonism of class interests, of wages and profits, of profits and rent, the starting-point of his investigations, naively taking this antagonism for a social law of nature. But with this contribution the bourgeois science of economics had reached the limits beyond which it could not pass ... In France and England the bourgeoisie had conquered political power. From that time on, the class struggle took on more and more explicit and threatening forms, both in practice and in theory. It sounded the knell of scientific bourgeois economics. It was thenceforth no longer a question whether this or that theorem was true, but whether it was useful to capital or harmful, expedient or inexpedient, in accordance with police regulations or contrary to them. In place of disinterested inquirers there stepped hired prize fighters; in place of genuine scientific research, the bad conscience and the evil intent of apologetics.[19]

---

18   Engels 1884, p. 98.
19   Marx 1990, pp. 96–7.

Grossman dealt with this historical development with such detail in order to simultaneously tease out the differences between Marx and classical economics, not out of any intrinsic interest, but in order to stress the special role that use-value plays in Marx's analysis and which had been nearly-completely neglected or overlooked in previous marxist accounts. As with bourgeois economics, marxist theoreticians have mostly focused on exchange-value, even though they knew that value has a dual-character as exchange- and use-value. Actually, use-values play no role in the capitalist economy; they are a means to an end, a means to utilise capital, to convert surplus-value into an enlarged exchange-value. For Marx, nonetheless, the dual-character of commodities had fundamental meaning, since the capitalist economy, its development, and its eventual demise rest on the difference between the use-value and exchange-value of labour power.

The narrow focus on exchange-value eventually restricted bourgeois economics to an analysis of price relations, such as are found in the market-place. Because prices cannot be explained by means of prices, a psychological underpinning was introduced into marginal utility theory. It was the goal of this school to substitute a subjective value theory in place of the one supplied by the classical economists and criticised by Marx. In marginal utility theory, values were attributed to the psychologically justified marginal utility of goods, as determined by demand. Use-value once again became a focal point, although not in its material form but rather as a psychological phenomenon. According to W.S. Jevons, for example, all economic laws can be reduced to the opposition between desire and pain. Because people strive to increase pleasure and avoid pain, both emotions can be seen as determinants that are accessible to mathematical calculations. Although ideas about the measurability of subjective values were soon abandoned, the theory is still used today.

It was not only for apologetic needs that economic theory remained caught within bourgeois ideology, but also the wish to rank economics among the positive sciences that sought an ahistorical and 'universal' theory of the economy, through which its apologetic aspects come into even sharper expression. Not the historically given relations of production, but people singly or in social exchange, determine the economy through the attempt to attain the greatest possible satisfaction of their needs. This idea found application throughout the economic system and led to a theory of equilibrium as a final consequence of all the individual attempts to attain the greatest utility. Equilibrium theory had a statistical aspect and assumed that imbalances would provoke price movements to re-establish that equilibrium.

Grossman followed this theory in all its changes and came to the conclusion that, overlooking other considerations, its statistical character was alone sufficient in order to demonstrate its indefensibleness. Because capitalism is a dynamic system, it makes no sense to research the principles of an imaginary statistical economy. A theory based solely on exchange-value also remains unreceptive to the issue of dynamism. Because this dynamic nonetheless constitutes reality, bourgeois theory had no choice but to explain this too. All attempts to do so, however, have failed. The unveiling of capitalism's developmental laws and their effect on the market mechanism remains reserved for marxism.

The idea of a self-regulating economy – one that tends towards equilibrium by means of the price mechanism – had already broken down in the Great Depression of 1929. Since then, deliberate attempts to intervene in the market mechanism have been necessary not only to guarantee increased production, but also to push forward the capitalisation of the world. As in the past, these attempts are based exclusively on market occurrences and therefore maintain their static character. Production is 'driven' by demand; no longer exclusively by consumers, but also through an increased demand through state expenditures that heightens 'public consumption'. Once again, the specific dynamic and the relations of production from which it results are left out of consideration.

In Keynes's methodologically static theory, crises originate in an imputed psychological law of declining consumption that sets in with enhanced wealth. Because production depends on consumption in this theory, the rate of investment declines. What that means in the long run is indeed mentioned but then promptly forgotten, since a crisis can be counteracted in the short term, and in Keynes's opinion, avoided altogether. With a decline in investment, systemwide equilibrium is coupled with unemployment. Within this system, it is impossible to restore full employment. That must occur through governmental interventions that heighten demand. If these are successful, a situation of equilibrium with full employment results. Nothing about the system has been altered; equilibrium is restored on another level.

Keynes was not aware of the consequences of this process, since he viewed the economy solely from the market aspect. But behind the market appearances exists the production of surplus-value. The goal of production is not consumption, but the accumulation of capital. Production declines when it is unprofitable. Production can only be expanded through a rate of surplus-value sufficient for further accumulation and which counteracts the fall in the rate of profit. Whatever is consumed cannot be accumulated, from which it follows that consumption is dependent on accumulation.

An increase in demand alone cannot provide a solution for crises, whereas an enhanced sum of surplus-value can once again push forward the accumulation process. A crisis finds its causes and its solutions in the sphere of production, insofar as solutions are possible. A conscious increase in demand that leads only to an enhanced production but not to further accumulation, will not be regarded as a remedy for crises, even though it increases economic activity. An enlarged production, by means of an expansion of the credit system, merely postpones but alters nothing in regard to the ongoing decline of the capitalist system.

Given that boom conditions have existed in the capitalistically developed countries since the Second World War, this finding may seem peculiar.[20] It was the combination of destruction, technological development, and conscious intervention into the economy that transformed the distinctive crisis conditions of the pre-war years into a new prosperity. The destruction of capital is a precondition for a further accumulation. Technical development furthers the production of surplus-value, and interventions into the economy reduced unemployment at the cost of the entire society. It begins to appear as if capitalism will be successful in eliminating its crisis tendencies. That this can only be an illusion results from an unaltered system of unaltered relations of production. Grossman's work again becomes actual because of its convincing demonstration of how capitalism's contradictions can only disappear with capitalism itself. The marxian analysis of capitalism has never been more necessary than today, because the system at no time has been as misunderstood as under its current conditions of existence.

---

20   Editor's Note: This essay was written in 1969, that is, just prior to the collapse of the international order and reorganisation of the global economy.

CHAPTER 9

Value Theory and Capital Accumulation

Marx's theory of capital development evolved out of his criticism of the value theory of *laissez-faire* capitalism.* In order to yield regulatory results, the market automatism presupposes a principle on which exchange is based, a principle that explains prices and their changes. A given price may vary in the interplay of supply and demand, but the question of what determines price remains. For the classicists, price was a derivation of value and value was determined by the socially necessary labour-time incorporated in commodities. There was no need to quarrel with this explanation which did not exclude specific cases where price has no relation to labour-time. At any rate, Marx accepted the labour theory of value as the closest approximation to the actual evaluation process which underlies prices.

For Marx, the inherent contradictions of capital production are not of an 'economic' character in the bourgeois sense of the term. He is concerned not with the supply and demand relations of the market but with the effect of the social forces of production upon the social relations of production, that is, with the results of the increasing productivity of labour upon the production of value and surplus-value. Celebrated as the product of capital itself, bourgeois theory separates growing productivity from its social implications. For Marx, it is the independent variable that determines all the other variables in the system of economic relationships.

Whatever the regulative power of competition and whatever the force of supply and demand may be, all that matters in the end, and from the point of view of development, is the changing productivity of labour. It transforms society materially and the material changes affect all socio-economic relations. This special importance of labour and its increasing productivity in Marx's scheme of reasoning led to the discovery of a definite developmental trend in capital accumulation which revealed qualitative changes in the wake of quantitative ones. He could show that the capitalist 'equilibrium mechanism' must itself change in the course of capital accumulation and that it is the latter which determines and modifies the market force of supply and demand, since the market laws have to assert themselves within a larger frame of a developing

---

* Notes on Joseph M. Gillman's *The Falling Rate of Profit: Marx's Law and Its Significance to Twentieth-Century Capitalism* (New York, 1958).

'disequilibrium' between the social forces of production and the capitalist relations of production.

As an explanation of the developmental tendencies of capital production, Marx found the theory of value indispensable and, in fact, the only 'rational basis of political economy'. He knew, of course, that the social labour process itself has nothing to do with either value or price but only with the time-consuming physical and mental exertions of the labouring population and that 'value' and 'price' are fetishistic categories for existing social production relations. It would not do, however, merely to point out that the ruling economic categories were themselves in need of explanation and that the whole 'science' of bourgeois economy could only make the perfectly clear requirements of social production and distribution obscure. In order to construct a theory of capital development, it was necessary to agree to the validity of a definite regulatory principle – the value concept – which came nearest to reality by expressing actual necessities and by incorporating the existing equilibrium tendencies of the market mechanism.

From the standpoint of the labour theory of value, the exchange-value of a commodity decreases with the increasing productivity of labour. However, capitalist production is production of exchange-value by way of the production of commodities. Its goal is surplus-value as additional exchange-value. Surplus-value is the difference between the exchange-value of labour power and its actual productive capacity. It is the time relation between the labour necessary to sustain and reproduce workers and the labour that falls to capitalists in the form of surplus-products realised in profits. Viewed capitalistically, a mere increase in productivity is senseless unless it involves an increase in surplus-value. The latter is made possible by an increase in productivity but implies a change in the relation between necessary and surplus-labour. More of the latter falls to the capitalists, less of the former to the workers.

The increase in productivity and surplus-value and the accumulation of capital are all one and the same process. It implies a more rapid growth of capital invested in means of production than that invested in labour power. In *Capital*, Marx constructs a value-model of capital development comprising the theoretically conceivable entity of 'total capital' with its social aggregates of wages, profits, and investments. The social reproduction process is here the accumulation of capital, that is, it implies reproduction on a larger scale. Capital invested in labour power Marx called 'variable capital' because of its ability to create surplus-value and thus additional capital. Capital invested in means of production he called 'constant capital'. The relation between these two parts, both with regard to their technical side and their value side he called the 'organic composition of capital'. Accumulation means a rising organic composition of capital, that is, more constant, less variable capital. As profits are calculated on the total invested capital, they must show a tendency to decline as that part of the total which alone yields surplus-value becomes relatively smaller. But the process also implies an increasing ability to extract more surplus-value, thus nullifying the 'tendency' of profits to decline, and constituting the reason for the process itself. According to Marx, then, the development of the social productivity of labour in capitalism expresses itself 'on the one hand in a tendency to a progressive fall of the rate of profit, and on the other hand in a progressive increase of the absolute mass of the appropriated surplus-value, or profit; so that on the whole a relative decrease of variable capital and profits is accompanied by an absolute increase of both. This twofold effect can express itself only in the growth of the total capital at a ratio more rapid than that expressed by the fall of the rate of profit'.[1]

The 'abstract law' that the growing productivity of labour manifests itself in a falling rate of profit simultaneously compensated for by an increasing mass of surplus-value may appear quite meaningless so long as capitalists are able to accumulate. However, the absence of a falling rate of profit in reality does not invalidate a value-scheme of capital development in which the rate of profit shows such a decline. To show this decline, to be sure, it is necessary to assume a capitalist system with a rising organic composition of capital and a static rate of exploitation, or, when a growing rate of surplus-value is considered, to assume a closed system with a given labour force in which the continuous accumulation process, demanding always more surplus-labour, brings the necessary labour towards zero. These are unrealistic conditions. What is real, nevertheless, is the accumulation process and the rising organic composition of capital. And although capitalists are not aware of a tendential fall of the rate of profit, they do suffer periods of declining profitability, and these periods are characterised by a decreasing rate of accumulation. By itself, this fact neither supports nor contradicts Marx's theory. It merely resembles the value-scheme of development. On the basis of his own assumption, the value-scheme of accumulation only postulates 'the possibility of crisis by a mere consideration of the general nature of capital, without regard to the additional and real relations that form the conditions of the real production process'.[2]

In the real world of capital production, it cannot be expected that capitalism will collapse because of accumulation, or, what amounts to the same thing, because of the tendential fall of the rate of profit. The end of accumulation

---

1 Marx 1909, p. 261.
2 Marx 1905b, p. 264.

could result only when real social conditions exclude a sufficient increase of surplus-value for a further expansion of capital or when the expansion of capital has reached a point where any further capital growth would yield the same, or less, surplus-value than before. As neither of these situations is predictable from the actual conditions of capital production, Rosa Luxemburg was quite right in considering that the idea that capitalism would collapse as a result of the falling rate of profit was too far-fetched. In her opinion 'a collapse of capitalism due to the falling rate of profit would take a very long time, probably just as long as the cooling-down of the sun'.[3]

Luxemburg's remarks, although true, are quite beside the point. For the 'self-liquidation' of capital production – by way of a falling rate of profit as implied in the value-model of capital expansion – was meant to lead toward an understanding of the actual process of capital formation and does not represent the latter only in a more generalised form. Marx, at any rate, never tired of pointing out that no predictions regarding the actual world can be based directly on the value-scheme of capital development. All real crises of capitalism must, in his view, be explained out of the empirically given condition, 'out of the real movement of capitalist production, competition, and credit'.[4]

Marx's theory of accumulation has no immediate and direct connection with the actual process of capital formation. The distinction between the value-model and reality must always be kept clear. Questions arising in the model cannot be answered with phenomena that appear only in reality, and solutions of problems of the actual world are not found in the value-scheme of development. The abstract value-scheme of capital expansion has its purpose, nevertheless. It indicates that, apart from competition as the driving force of capital development in the market reality, the production and accumulation of surplus-value finds in the twofold character of capital production (use- and exchange-value) a limiting element, to be overcome only by a continuous expansion and extension of capital and the capitalist mode of production. According to Marx, capitalism's basic contradiction consists in the conflict between the expansion of production and the creation of value. It consists, generally speaking, in the fact 'that the capitalist mode of production has a tendency to develop the productive forces absolutely, regardless of the value and of the surplus-value contained in it and regardless of the social conditions under which capitalist production takes place; while it has on the other hand for its aim the preservation of the value of the existing capital and its

---

3 Luxemburg 1921, p. 38.
4 Marx 1905a, p. 286.

self-expansion to the highest limit'.[5] An unconditional development of production under the auspices of competition can lead to a situation where the expansion of use-values would no longer correspond to the value-expansion of capital and, for that reason, would temporarily end. It is in this sense that Marx proclaims that 'the real barrier to capitalist production is capital itself. It is the fact that capital and its self-expansion appear as the starting and closing point, as the motive aim of production ... which steer straight toward an unrestricted extension of production. The means, this unconditional development of the productive forces of society, comes continually into conflict with the limited end, the self-expansion of the existing capitals'.[6]

In Marx's abstract value-scheme, accumulation leads to a final lack of surplus-value when certain limiting conditions of expansion are assumed. Although these assumed conditions will not arise in reality, it is quite clear that for all capitals, all national capitals and for the whole of capitalism there do exist at any particular time definite limits to their profitable expansion. And it is not the market alone, but the whole social situation in all its ramifications which, at times, constitutes a limit to capital expansion. As it is not possible to calculate when the expansion of one or all capitals reaches its limits in actual social conditions, limiting conditions had to be assumed in order to reveal the meaning of the process here involved.

Over-accumulation of capital is always the endpoint of a period of accumulation wherein the extension of production parallels the expansion of capital. When existing conditions of exploitation preclude a further profitable capital expansion, a crisis sets in. This, of course, leads to processes that remove the temporary barrier to further accumulation. But the reorganisation of the total capital structure here involved sets new limits within the new conditions characteristic for another period. There is, however, no reason to assume that the conditions of production will always change so as to accommodate the need for capital expansion; the less so, as the conditions of production are the general social conditions of production and the need for capital expansion is a particular need bound to nothing but the exploitative capital-labour relationship.

Marx's abstract theory of capital development, though incapable of predicting the definite end of capitalism, is significant as an instrument to be set against the persistent illusion that capitalism could actually reach that state of tranquillity held out by its apologists as the only hope of the future. It helps explain why all the concrete contradictions encountered in reality cannot be

---

5 Marx 1909, p. 292.
6 Marx 1909, p. 293.

considered accidental or remediable shortcomings. These difficulties, singly and as a developmental pattern, are due to a trend in capital accumulation itself. When capitalism's inner connections are grasped, Marx wrote, 'all theoretical belief in the permanent necessity of existing conditions breaks down before their practical collapse'.[7] The vagueness of his theory was both its weakness and its strength, but above all, it was the only form in which capitalist development could be comprehended.

1 The Falling Rate of Profit and Its Counter-Tendencies

There are marxists who have projected Marx's findings with regard to the value-model of capital expansion into the real world of capital formation. And it must be admitted that Marx, and his editor, did not always distinguish clearly enough between the real world of capitalism and its appearance in value theory. But while, in the case of Marx, this may be considered a literary shortcoming, for some of his disciples the 'law of value', as the economic counterpart to the dialectics, seems to assure the breakdown of capitalism.[8] Marx's critique of political economy became the ideology of the inevitability of socialism. As such, the theory of breakdown waxed and waned with the capitalist movement from depression to prosperity, from relative stability to the general crisis. While in vogue, however, it was always admitted that the contradictory value production, which turns the drive for profits into their decline, has no counterpart in immediate reality. Capitalism's basic tendency, it was argued, is offset by counter-tendencies. But as all these counter-tendencies are supposedly over-ruled by the 'law of value', they were thought to exhaust themselves in the course of time and the as yet unnoticeable fall of the rate of profit would become a real decline and destroy the capitalist system.

Gillman's book raises the question of the falling rate of profit for contemporary capitalism. He points out that this question has hitherto 'been argued mainly on theoretical grounds', which, of course, is the only ground it can be argued on. Gillman, however, attempts to deal with it on 'both theoretical and historical-statistical grounds', and there he finds that 'for the years before about World War I the historical statistics seem fully to support these theories of Marx; after that war the series studied appear generally to behave in contradiction to the marxist expectations'. Gillman wonders whether his procedure

---

7 Marx 1973b, p. 74.
8 For instance: Grossmann 1970.

and statistics are wrong, or whether Marx was right for the period of competitive capitalism and wrong for the period of monopoly capitalism; particularly 'with respect to the counter-tendencies which became effective as offsets to the falling tendency of the rate of profit in this (monopoly) period'.

Gillman's re-formulation of Marx's 'law of the falling rate of profit', is, unfortunately, a misstatement, for he asserts that the rate of profit falls 'because the drive toward unlimited capital accumulation tends to delimit the capitalistically-determined consumer market potentials wherein alone profits can be realized' (4).[9] In Marx's theory, however, the rate of profit falls even on the assumption that there is no realisation problem. It is a question of the expansion of production and the expansion of value, not of its realisation. The realisation of surplus-value is a problem of the concrete market situation, not of abstract value analysis. But here at the very outset, as well as throughout his book, Gillman moves from abstract value analysis into concrete production and distribution relations, and *vice versa*, unaware that such procedures are not permissible. And thus he does not notice that his distinction between competitive and monopoly capitalism has no bearing on the tendential fall of the rate of profit, as the latter refers to 'total capital', disregards issues of monopoly and competition and assumes validity for all stages of capital development. Finally, and in contrast to those theoreticians who waited for the counter-tendencies to the falling rate of profit to exhaust themselves, Gillman points out that it may be a question of the varying effectiveness of these counter-tendencies which will explain why there was an actual fall of the rate of profit in an earlier period of capital expansion and why this no longer holds true for present-day capitalism.

According to Marx, 'the same causes which produce a falling tendency in the rate of profit, also call forth counter-effects, which check and partly paralyze this fall'.[10] Counter-tendencies to the tendential fall of the rate of profit as listed by Marx include the rising intensity of exploitation, the depression of wages below their value, the cheapening of the elements of constant capital, relative overpopulation, foreign trade, and the increase of stock capital.[11] To speak about a 'tendential decline of the profit-rate' and of 'counter-tendencies' to this decline, means to speak simultaneously in terms of value analysis and concrete reality. This is permissible if one keeps in mind that only the 'counter-tendencies' are real phenomena and reveal by their existence the unobservable tendential fall of the profit rate. Moreover, Marx's 'counter-tendencies' may

---

9 Numbers in parentheses refer to pages in Gillman's book.
10 Marx 1909, p. 280.
11 Marx 1909, pp. 272–82.

combat an actual fall of profit rates – may bolster, or even increase, a given rate of profit, quite independent of the 'tendential fall of the rate of profit' associated with the rising organic composition of capital.

The 'counter-effects' listed by Marx have no direct connection with the abstract theory of the falling rate of profit; they merely indicate the disorder and incompleteness which are characteristic of the last volume of *Capital*, published as it was long after Marx's death. The rise of exploitation and the cheapening of constant capital are not properly 'counter-tendencies' to the tendential fall of the rate of profit. They are distinguishable from the latter only in the sense that the two phases of the cardiac cycle are distinguishable – that is, as the singular movement of capital accumulation. That a rising organic composition of capital should lead to a relative overpopulation is quite clear, but this relative over-population can hardly serve as a 'counter-tendency' to the falling rate of profit. It does so, according to Marx, because it brings forth new employment in industries with low organic capital composition and thus raises the average rate of profit. But the competitive process which brings about the average rate of profit has no place in Marx's abstract value analysis, dealing as it does, with total capital. For this reason, 'foreign trade' must also be excluded, not to speak of 'wages below their value' and the 'increase of stock capital' in a theory based on the law of value. In reality, of course, new industries with low organic compositions are installed, some workers are paid below their value, and foreign trade is often highly profitable. But these items are meaningful only in connection with the actual movement of capital, not with the general theory of accumulation based on the law of value.

The 'counter-tendencies' mentioned by Marx either retard the growing organic composition of capital, increase the rate of surplus-value, or have both effects simultaneously. What, then, becomes of the 'law of the falling rate of profit'? Marx gives no answer; neither does Gillman. The latter turns, instead, to the statistical test of the 'law'. He notices, of course, that 'the available statistics are not in the form exactly suited to the purpose' – an understatement if there ever was one – for 'capitalist business firms do not report, nor do official statistical agencies process their statistics to conform to the marxist categories'. Nor could they, one may add, even if they tried since price-relations are not direct derivations of value-relations. Above all, Gillman points out, 'these statistics do not allow us to separate out the factors which affect the production of surplus-value from those which affect its realisation, as a full test of the law as Marx formulated it would require'. However, 'with this precaution in mind', he thinks that 'they can be made to serve as fair approximations for testing the assumptions which underlie the law' (31).

Since we have no intention of questioning Gillman's statistical compilations, we will only repeat their results, namely, that for American capitalism and up to 1919, Marx's 'law' found empirical evidence in 'a stabilising tendency of the rate of surplus-value, and a falling rate of profit corresponding inversely with a rising organic composition' (59). Apparently, Marx knew more than he was able to express or was, perhaps, just lucky in assuming an actual fall of the rate of profit in the long run. On the other hand, the declining profit rate, as detected by Gillman's statistical procedure, may have nothing to do with Marx's 'law of the falling rate of profit' as a consequence of the rising organic composition of capital, but may be a localised peculiarity of American capital development, quite independent of the 'general law of capital accumulation'. There is no way of finding out, and thus the evaluation of Gillman's data remains a matter of interpretation. It depends on various preconceptions with regard to capital formation whether the data are read as 'proof' of the validity of Marx's 'law', or as 'proof' of its opposite. For instance, if the 'law' ceases to be operative in 1919, one can easily maintain that, after all, only at that time did American capitalism come properly into its own, so that the period prior to this date may be considered as one beset with all the difficulties in the way of an unfolding capitalism, which, in spite of a rapid growth of its organic composition, has not as yet the possibility of fully partaking of its created surplus-value. Because the creation and the division of surplus-value, internally as well as internationally, are two different processes, and because, as Gillman points out, his statistics do not separate the production of surplus-value from its realisation, the falling rate of profit – as seen in the returns of American business – provides no clue to the question of whether or not there was a fall of the rate of profit in Marx's sense.

There are various specific reasons which limited the profitability of American capital under the conditions of the nineteenth-century world-market and the dominance of European capitalism. And, contrary to Gillman, the 'countertendencies' to a falling rate of profit were more effective at that time than later. For the rapid rise of the organic composition of capital was indicative of a rapid increase of surplus-value by way of both the shortening of the necessary- and the lengthening of the surplus-labour time. While it may be said that the counteracting effect of foreign trade on the falling rate of profit was less efficient in an early stage of development than in the stage of American imperialism, all that has been said is that at this earlier time it was correspondingly more efficient for the European economies at the expense of American capital. World capital would come nearest to the concept of 'total capital', to which the falling rate of profit relates itself, yet the unavailable data for world capitalism, if they were available, would be just as irrelevant to the problem of the falling rate of profit as the historical-statistical material presented for American capitalism.

According to Gillman, however, as far as American monopoly-capitalism is concerned, this is a thing of the past. The same statistical procedure that first yielded a rising organic composition and a falling rate of profit also shows that, since 1919, the ratio between constant and variable capital 'has tended to remain constant or even fall. The rate of surplus-value, if anything, has tended to rise, in spurts. And the rate of profit, rather than fall, has tended to rise' (59). This supposedly contradicts Marx's 'law', but rather than say that Marx was wrong with regard to American monopoly capitalism, Gillman takes the view 'that the traditional formula ... to demonstrate the operation of the law is not valid under these new conditions ... because its terms ... are too rigid to encompass and reflect the effects of the new technology and the new forms of business organizations on the production as well as on the realization of surplus-value' (60–1).

The changes which Gillman refers to consist in 'the maturation of the institution of monopoly capitalism; the revolution in the technology of production, which advanced the productivity of labour without requiring comparably large additions of the constant capital; and the increasing cost of doing business – the increasing cost of the realization of surplus-value in its first form, that is, in the form of money capital through the sale of commodities' (67). After World War I, so Gillman relates, industry concentrated 'on the elimination of waste; on the standardization of parts, products, and processes; on improving the efficiency of plants and labour, and on the development of by-products' (75). And whereas it can be pointed out that this 'rationalisation' had been going on all along, according to Gillman, it has now led to a 'qualitative change in the nature of constant capital, which was concealed by its traditional quantitative expression' (80). Capital-saving and labour-saving devices raised the rate of surplus-value without increasing the organic composition of capital, thus setting aside the law of the falling rate of profit. But as the new technology 'tends to minimize the consumption of raw materials per unit of output and to prolong the life of the fixed capital in terms of product output, it tends also in the long run to minimize the demand for investment capital ... and create a new market problem ... and intensifies the problem of the realization of surplus-value' (81). In brief, the apparent end of the capitalist dilemma posed by the tendential fall of the rate of profit only intensifies other problems and creates new difficulties unsolvable under conditions of capital production.

'Marxists', according to Gillman, 'have tended to treat the problem of the falling rate of profit chiefly in terms of the rate of creation of surplus-value'. But 'from a statistical or factual research point of view', he says, 'it must be asserted that the amount of surplus-value created exists only in so far as it is realized' (86). And as realisation of surplus-value 'is increasingly impossible without the services of clerks and salesmen and advertising writers, and of government ... these 'unproductive' services ... are essential to the functioning of the system' (88). Whereas by a mere consideration of surplus-value production 'the tendencies postulated by the marxist law of the falling rate of profit appear to be halted or even reversed, by a consideration of the growth of the 'unproductive' as against the productive labour the original tendencies are seen to re-assert themselves' (104). There is then a falling rate of profit, after all, despite the new technology and the new business organisations; only it relates itself not to the production but to the realisation of surplus-value. 'Overhead' eats up the profit.

According to Gillman, then, the solution of the problem of the falling rate of profit 'would seem to lie in the interaction of the antagonistic forces which govern the creation and realization of surplus-value' (108). Although this is not Marx's point of view, it is also not true from Gillman's position, for he does not really refer to the 'realisation' of surplus-value but merely to its division. When the increasing productivity of labour does not find expression in the accumulation of capital, a crisis results – there is a glut on the commodity market and large-scale unemployment. The surplus-value incorporated in commodities cannot be 'realised', that is, turned into additional capital. But if there is relative capital stagnation and simultaneously no glut on the commodity market and no large-scale unemployment, it is clear that surplus-value, though not realised in additional capital, has been realised in another form – that of 'unproductive' consumption. It can be argued that this situation results from capitalism's inability to raise the rate of accumulation. It can also be argued, as the capitalists generally do, that this division of surplus-value hinders the accumulation of capital, for which reason they are in constant struggle to cut 'overhead' and reduce 'government spending'. But in either case, and regardless of underlying reasons, this is more a question of the division than of the realisation of surplus-value.

To be sure, Gillman is aware of the fact that unproductive expenditures 'tend to ease the disposal of consumer goods and the realization of surplus-value as money-capital', which, then, 'tend to lower the rate of the net profit' (131). In other words, the profits of productive capital decline even though the social mass of surplus-value rises and is partly 'realised' by way of unproductive consumption and waste production. The fall of the rate of profit, so to speak, affects not capitalist society but the capitalists. They had no chance under *laissez-faire* conditions because of rapid capital accumulation which brings the rate of profit down, and they have no chance now, for the decline of the rate of accumulation also brings down the rate of profit. It is, then, not really a question of antagonism between the production and the realisation of surplus-value, but of a change of capitalism itself, which, because it can no longer accumulate progressively to private account, changes into a society increasingly less oriented to production of capital and more oriented towards production for consumption. What bourgeois theory had always claimed, and what Marx and the marxists had always denied, namely, that capitalist production is production for consumption, is now in the process of being factually decided in favour of the former through the evolution of capitalism 'as a consumption economy'. Not only has the 'law of the falling rate of profit' led to monopoly capitalism and the new technology, but at this monopolistic stage, the 'falling rate of profit' indicates the eventual end of capital production. The greater effectiveness of the prevailing counter-tendencies to the falling rate of profit, which changed the nature of constant capital qualitatively, proved, in the end, more disastrous to capital than the rise of the organic composition of capital when accompanied by less effective counter-tendencies. On this note, Gillman's book ends, leaving the problems of 'capitalism as a consumption economy' to another, forthcoming work.

2 Accumulation, Crises and Depressions

We did not bother to check Gillman's statistical evidence because, while they are wanting in many important respects, we think them quite irrelevant to the problems under discussion. We will assume that both his procedure and the statistics are flawless and that it is a 'statistically verifiable fact' that there was a drop in the rate of profit in the course of American capital development up to 1919, and that since that time there has again been such a drop when the 'unproductively' realised surplus-value is deducted from the total surplus-value. Against this statistical evidence, however, there stands the no less factual truth that American capitalism did accumulate not only up to 1919 but up to the present, as manifested by its vast productive apparatus. The accumulation process was, of course, interrupted by various crises and depressions. But when these periods of stagnation and decline are left aside by, say, a consideration of the yearly average rate of expansion over the last hundred years, it becomes evident that these hundred years were a period of steady expansion of production and capital.

Although Gillman was not able to find a direct statement by Marx as to why the rate of profit must fall in the long run, he states nevertheless that 'the cyclical fall of the rate of profit is in itself a consequence of the maturation of several tendencies which, in dialectical interaction with its long-run tendency to fall, generate the periodic breakdown of capitalist production' (6). This connection between the 'long-run' tendency of the rate of profit to fall and periodic crises is also to be found in Marx, even though it does not necessarily follow from his abstract value analysis of capital accumulation, which can only point out that under certain assumed conditions accumulation comes to a halt because of a lack of surplus-value relative to total capital. Such a situation may not arise in reality; yet it may arise by an expansion of production which 'out-runs' the profit claims associated with it and yields surplus-value, which, however large, is not large enough to assure a further profitable capital expansion. What possible meaning could the 'law of the falling rate of profit' have with regard to the actual accumulation process if it did not serve to indicate the possibility of an increasing lack of surplus-value and a consequent disruption of the accumulation process? In Gillman's view, however, 'capitalism is in crisis ... because it produces too much surplus-value for its ultimate realization in the progressive accumulation of productive capital' (126).

This, too, of course, is true in a sense, but it does not contradict Marx's position that it is primarily a question of the production not the realisation of surplus-value which accounts for the contradictions of the accumulation process. It is clear that the increasing mass of surplus-value in commodity form must be sold, and that if it cannot be sold it cannot be realised in additional capital. The discrepancy between the creation of surplus-value and its realisation appears, as has already been pointed out, as a glut on the commodity market, as an overproduction of commodities. Seen from the angle of productive development rather than its results, the overproduction of commodities appears as an overproduction of capital. But the distinction between them is important. For the overproduction of capital (including that of commodities), instead of leading to a curtailment of productivity only accelerates it, thereby indicating that the discrepancy between the production of surplus-value and its realisation arises because of a decline in the rate of accumulation. With a sufficient rate of accumulation, there would be no overproduction and, in fact, as soon as the expansion process is resumed, the market becomes once more what is considered 'normal', despite the even larger quantities of commodities now offered for sale. What is involved here is not, then, an overproduction of commodities either in relation to the absolute consuming power of society, or the relative consuming power in capitalism, but an overproduction of commodities in relation to the capitalistically limited demand under the particular conditions of relative capital stagnation. Of course, the reason for this stagnation may be the impossibility of converting the mass of surplus-value from its commodity-form into a surplus-value-producing capital form. But it may also be the other way around: the conversion cannot take place because of the stagnation of capital. The first possibility springs from the fact that the buying and selling of commodities and the creation of surplus-value are separated logically as well as by time and space. An overproduction of commodities may thus only express disproportionalities in the development of the market structure. Marx did not deny that overproduction may be caused by such disproportionalities, but more important to him was the consideration of the other possibility, namely, that the overproduction of commodities signifies an overproduction, or over-accumulation, of capital.

For Marx, the barrier to capitalist production consists in the fact 'that the development of the productive power of labour creates in the falling rate of profit a law which turns into an antagonism of this mode of production at a certain point and requires for its defeat periodical crises. In the fact that the expansion or contraction of production is determined by the appropriation of unpaid labour, and by the proportion of this unpaid labour to materialised labour in general, or, to speak the language of the capitalists, is determined by profit and by the proportion of this profit to the employed capital, by a definite rate of profit, instead of being determined by the relations of production to social wants .... The capitalist mode of production, for this reason, meets with barriers at a certain scale of production which would be inadequate under different conditions. It comes to a standstill at a point determined by the production and realization of profit, not by the satisfaction of social needs'.[12] This situation, the relative overproduction of capital, involving the overproduction of commodities and thus the realisation problem, means that accumulation has reached a point where the profits associated with it are no longer large enough to justify further expansion. There is no incentive to invest and because there is no new, or no substantial new, investment of capital, the demand for all commodities declines. The resulting general lack of demand appears as the overproduction of commodities, and this apparent overproduction suggests the realisation problem as the cause of crisis.

To be sure, from the angle of market occurrences, there actually exists this realisation problem, the overproduction of commodities, and the decline of capitalistically determined consuming power. And there is also the certainty that by increasing the consuming power and thus avoiding the commodity glut, no realisation problem could arise and the production process could be resumed; provided, of course, capitalism would not be capitalism. But even under capitalist conditions and after a period of depression, overproduction and the realisation problem disappear in a new upswing through resumed capital accumulation, of which the accompanying increase of consumption is just

---

12   Marx 1909, p. 303.

a by-product and not its reason. To show the mechanism of relative overproduction of capital, Marx assumed conditions of an absolute overproduction of capital in his value-scheme of capital expansion wherein the rising organic composition of capital destroys the profitability of capital.

Under capitalism there is no way of determining at what particular developmental point capital expansion will conflict with the principle of profitability and thus reduce the rate of accumulation. With a given satisfactory or rising rate of profit, all capitals attempt expansion. And because this expansion goes on without regard to and knowledge of existing, though undeterminable, social limits of exploitation, the increased exploitation implied in the expansion process, whatever it may be, may not suffice to yield a mass of surplus-value indicating a rate of profit on the enlarged total capital equal to a previous rate of profit of a smaller total capital. New investments, oriented to the rate of profit, will fall off or stop altogether and a period of depression will set in. Whether an actual fall of the rate of profit through a relative overexpansion of capital can be regarded as the 'cause' of crisis is to be seen not in the crisis itself but in the period of depression, which prepares the way for the resumption of the accumulation process.

During periods of depression attempts are made to bring the production process once again into harmony with the value-expansion process. Just as the crisis lays bare the discrepancy between material and value production and the approach of the crisis is signalised by a slackening rate of investment, overproduction, and unemployment, so the way out of the depression is effected by closing the gap between expansion and profitability, by a resulting increase of new investments and a consequent 'normalising' of the commodity and labour market. The periodicity of the crises stems from the ability of capitalism to overcome the relative overproduction of capital through an altering of the conditions of production.

A crisis does not just start but starts in certain industries, even though its cause lies in the total social situation. Like the crisis, the upswing, too, starts in certain industries and cumulatively affects the whole economy. Because capital accumulation is the enlarged reproduction of the means of production, the upswing and decline, although general, are first and foremost noticeable in the manufacture of production goods. The crisis, however, does not picture the real situation. Just as the upswing exaggerates profit expectations, so the crisis exaggerates declining profitability. In either direction the competitive process tends to extremes and hastens both the overproduction of capital and the reorganisation of the capital structure. The crisis itself is merely the point at which the reversal of business conditions is publicly recognised. A depression may 'sneak' into existence by a gradual slowing down of economic activity or it may be initiated by a dramatic 'crash' with sudden bank failures and the collapse of the stock market. Whatever the circumstances surrounding the reversal of the economic trend, it is accompanied by an overproduction of commodities. Viewed in retrospect, even the last phases of the boom preceding the crisis are already unprofitable, but recognition of this fact has to await the verdict of the market. Commitments made on the assumption of a continuous upward trend cannot be met. The conversion of capital from commodity to money form becomes increasingly more difficult. The crisis of production is a financial crisis. The need for liquid funds and the attempts to avoid greater losses intensify the fall of securities and commodity prices. Competition becomes generally cut-throat competition and, for some businesses, prices are forced down to the point of ruin. Capital values are rapidly depreciated, fortunes lost, incomes wiped out. Social demand further declines as the number of unemployed grows and the commodity glut is checked only by the still faster decline of production. The crisis extends into all spheres and branches of the economy and, in this general form, reveals the social interdependence of the capitalist mode of production despite private property relations which control its trend.

After a period of panic, however, the capitalist economy reorients itself towards a new stability under changed conditions. Capital values have been destroyed and depleted, profit claims have been considerably reduced and, though the productive apparatus has somewhat deteriorated by neglect and insufficient replacement, the great bulk of constant capital in its physical form has not been altered. The material-technical composition of capital is still largely the same, but its value-composition has been lowered. More use-value in the form of means of production represents now a smaller exchange-value. By counting for less without being less, the relationship between variable and total capital is more favourable as regards profitability. As before, a given quantity of the means of production will require a given quantity of labour, but from the viewpoint of value, the growing discrepancy between variable and constant capital has been arrested or reduced. Nothing has changed with regard to the productivity of labour and the rate of exploitation; yet, the profitability has been improved since the mass of surplus-value can now relate itself to a smaller value of total capital. The destruction of capital values concentrates capital in fewer hands; weaker capital entities sell out to the stronger, often at prices that have no relation to even the reduced value of the means of production or to the commodities that are being transferred. Capital entities able to weather the depression 'accumulate' means of production already accumulated by their former owners. What one capitalist loses, another gains. By itself this transfer of property is socially meaningless. But with regard to the future, it eases the recovery process. By increasing the productive capacity of the more stable corporations without increasing their value to the same degree, it increases their profitability.

Some kind of 'equilibrium' is thus established between the given scale of production and its profitability, which serves as a starting point for an upward business trend. The new 'foothold' thus gained is utilised, so to speak, to make some further steps in the direction of security by way of accumulation. Intensified competition and the decline of prices serve as incentives to increase productivity and to gain exceptional profits through the employment of new working techniques and new machinery. Prolonged depression makes possible a lowering of wages and a higher intensity of labour. In brief, the conditions of capital production become more favourable, the demand for capital begins to rise, and the cycle can run its course once more.

Despite intermittent periods of depression, each upswing of capital production reaches a higher point and wider extension than at its previous peak of development. There are fewer capitalists relative to the increased capital but more in absolute numbers. There are fewer workers employed relative to the accumulated capital but more in absolute numbers. Capital develops in a manner that may be described as three steps forward and two steps back. But this type of locomotion does not hinder the general advance, it only slows it up. Disregarding the hectic fluctuations of expansion and contraction, the many upheavals and social struggles that capital development involves, and looking at the whole capitalist development as a continuous and steady process, it appears that the rate of development is quite moderate. To speak, then, of the capitalist crisis or the 'business cycle' is merely to refer to the specific manner in which capital accumulates under competitive market conditions where the interrelations of capitalist production as a whole are left to their self-enforcement by way of crisis. As with any regulative mechanism in capitalism, the relationship between production and profitability must first be regulated (in order to regulate anything at all) and the competitive mechanism must, in the very process of general adjustment first re-establish or maintain a social average rate of profit that allows for the expansion of capital.

Although much more need be said about Marx's theory of accumulation, which is also a theory of crisis, what has already been said is sufficient to show that for Marx the capitalist problem is one of the production of surplus-value which determines the existence of the realisation problem and of the various market expressions of the crisis. Gillman may agree with this description of the so-called business-cycle as valid for the pre-monopolistic stage of capital development, even though it would contradict his reformulation of Marx's 'law of the falling rate of profit', which did not really refer to the contradiction inherent in capital accumulation but to the fact that capitalist production is not production for the satisfaction of human wants. And this, of course, is also true. When Marx states that the ultimate cause of all real crises 'remains the poverty and restricted consumption of the masses as compared to the tendency of capitalist production to develop the productive forces in such a way that only the absolute power of consumption of the entire society would be the limit',[13] this obvious discrepancy between production and consumption, though a condition of capitalist existence, does not alter the fact that it is also a contradiction between production and consumption. In Marx's view, the crisis cannot be abolished by either a reduction of production, an increase of consumption, nor by co-ordinating both. To co-ordinate both would be equivalent to ending capitalist production itself. Neither capitalist crisis nor capitalist prosperity causes or eliminates under-consumption or overproduction; they merely refer to more or less of both, in which a widening disequilibrium appears at times as an apparent equilibrium.

Gillman may point out that the 'qualitative' change of constant capital changes the crisis from one of relative and temporary overproduction of capital into one of absolute and permanent overproduction, as signified by a static, or declining, rate of accumulation, and that it is this new situation which does away with the problem of the production of surplus-value and raises the realisation problem to first place – to the capitalist problem *per se*. If this is so, Gillman is not dealing with the type of capitalism Marx dealt with, but with a new type of capitalism, no longer susceptible to marxian analysis. But why, then, bother with the 'falling rate of profit?' If it is true that 'the conditions which block the realization of surplus-value continue to drive surplus-value increasingly into channels of unproductive expenditures' (110), then you have increasingly less 'accumulation for the sake of accumulation' – which forms the marxian reason for the crisis – but, in always greater measure, production for consumption and waste. Whatever else it may be, this is not capitalist production in the traditional sense.

But is it really necessary to relate a 'qualitative' change of capitalism to a 'qualitative' change of constant capital? Even if constant capital is 'cheapened' by capital-saving new technology, and even if the mass of surplus-value is too large to be absorbed as additional capital in America, why can it not be realised somewhere else? For in the world at large there is no overproduction of capital, no capital-saving new technology and, most of all, no abundance of surplus-value. In reality, then, American capital is unable to realise its surplus-

---

13   Marx 1909, p. 568.

value in additional capital-producing capital not because of the new technology and the new business organisations, but because the expansion of capital finds limits in its national form of development. Without these national limits the realisation problem, as related by Gillman, would not exist and crises would once again be expressions of a developing discrepancy between material and value production. Violent attempts are then made to bridge national limitations to capital expansion at the expense of other nations. For the crisis now requires not only rationalisation of industry, capital destruction, concentration, and centralisation, but a general reorganisation of the economic and social structures on an international scale.

Capitalism is in crisis not because of an abundance of surplus-value but because it cannot raise the surplus-value short of reorganising the world capital structure. Economic depression as the 'equilibrating' force of capital production is no longer effective enough to create conditions for the resumption of capital accumulation on a progressive scale. The functions of depression are taken over by war and consequently by preparation for war, and, as in ordinary depression, the profitability of capital declines as a precondition for its later rise. It is still the mechanism underlying Marx's theory of accumulation. But whether it will once more succeed in creating favourable conditions for purposes of capital accumulation is not an 'economic' question but a question of social occurrences on a national and international scale. But, then, that was true for any period of crisis and depression, which always contained the possibility of social action aimed at ending all capitalist difficulties by ending the capitalist system.

Moreover, because no 'purely economic problems' exist, capitalist crisis conditions are, in part, partial transformations of capitalism, affecting its various social layers in different ways. Capital stagnation, combined with an extraordinary growth of surplus-value within a setting of ever-threatening war, allows some social groups to appropriate, or divert to themselves surplus-value which, under different conditions, would not be at their disposal. The extraordinary appropriation of surplus-value by unproductive layers of society is thus merely another indication of capitalism in crisis. And if this crisis should prove to be 'permanent' it will, in time, alter the whole social structure of capitalism.

This is also on Gillman's mind. 'When capitalist investment', he writes, 'must be increasingly geared to the expansion of consumption; when investment can no longer find its *raison d'être* in the accumulation of capital *per se*, then capitalism comes to the end of its 'historical mission' and must cease to grow as a system of social production' (156). But Gillman's very modification of Marx's 'law of the falling rate of profit' turns his description of the current capitalist dilemma into a type of Keynesian description in marxist terms. Like Keynes, Gillman speaks of a 'mature' capitalism and Keynes's 'liquidity preference' is Gillman's reduced rate of accumulation. Gillman's difficulties in the 'realisation' of surplus-value appear in Keynes as large-scale unemployment leading to government actions that increase non-productive consumption. Although Keynes favoured both an increased incentive to invest and an increased propensity to consume, in his view even the latter by itself provides the possibility of an escape from the conditions of unemployment by a partial break with the principle of profitability. However, what Keynes did not bother to say Gillman says, namely, that this process, if continued for long, must lead to the eventual destruction of private capital. Of course, Gillman connects the 'threat of conversion of capitalism into a consumption economy' with a constant capitalist 'struggle to escape crucifixion on the cross of a consumption economy', and with 'social, economic, political, and moral conflicts, national and international, which these and related conditions generate in time' (159). But from his position, pressure in the direction of the 'consumption economy' must continue to exert itself so that it is just a question of time when the 'accumulation for the sake of accumulation' comes to an end.

That the continuous increase of the so-called 'public sector' over the private sector of the economy will lead eventually to a form of state capitalism is to be expected. But the latter is not a 'consumption economy'. To be sure, 'consumption economy' does not mean an increase in the consuming power of the labouring population, although, according to Gillman, this is true to some extent. It means 'unproductive consumption' due to the growth of non-productive layers of society and 'consumption' by way of waste production, such as armaments. The underlying assumption that there is too much surplus-value for the expansion of productive capital allows, however, for another assumption, namely, that capitalist society can overcome its crisis by an accommodation to this new situation through government-directed distribution of surplus-value. This was indeed the argument of those Keynesians who pointed out that full employment, made possible by war and destruction, was equally possible under conditions of peace by channelling production into directions that increased the consuming power of society and its general welfare. However unrealistic these assumptions are in a 'mixed economy' still dominated by private capital, they do stem from the notion that capitalism finds itself in crisis because of an abundance of surplus-value. Gillman does not share the naivete of the Keynesians. Yet, on the basis of his theory, the solution to the socio-economic problems of today seems to lie in completing the deprivatisation of capital as the sole necessary medium for transforming the prevailing social production process into one in which not the accumulation of capital but the consumption requirements of society becomes the determining factor.

The trend to government control of the economy is, however, only another phase of the centralisation and concentration process of capital accumulation from *laissez-faire* capitalism to monopoly capitalism, and thence to state capitalism. And as the national character of state capitalism continues competitive production on an international scale, production in the state capitalist system is geared not to consumption but to international power struggles in various attempts to overcome national limits to the expansion of diverse national capitalisms. Moreover, by retaining the class relationship of controllers and controlled, state capitalism, to make itself possible, requires a continuation of proletarian conditions of existence for the working population. Production and distribution will consequently not be geared to social consumption but to the reproduction of the existing, though modified, class relationship. In other words, the ending of 'production for the sake of production' in 'planned state capitalism' does not involve the end of exploitative surplus-value production. After all, 'accumulation for the sake of accumulation' is only production for the capitalist class under fetishistic conditions of capital production. Getting rid of the fetishistic aspects of capital production still leaves production intact for capitalists, even though these 'capitalists' are no longer private owners of capital resources but organised plunderers of surplus-value by virtue of political control over the means of production.

CHAPTER 10

Marxism and Its Critics

The German edition of Joseph M. Gillman's *The Falling Rate of Profit* has provided him with an opportunity to respond to critics of the first English edition of the book. He also addresses my objections in a manner that makes it appropriate to quickly tackle these issues again. Gillman assumes that Marx's law of the falling rate of profit, like other scientific laws, can only be verified quantitatively. Otherwise, the law would be a pure abstraction without concrete application on the actual trends of capitalist development. He admits that neither Marx nor anyone else since 'has rigorously tested the law either empirically or historically'. In Marx's case, that is understandable since 'the appropriate data was not available with which the law could be tested'. That task was left until the present, whereby Gillman investigates 'whether the empirically-determined quantitative data agrees with the law's theoretical expectations'.

Gillman attempts to verify the law numerically, because he is convinced that behind the marxian categories of constant capital, variable capital, and surplus-value, exist real, statistically determinable magnitudes. He attempts to demonstrate this with data drawn from key sectors of the American economy. In my opinion, the available data tells us nothing about movements in the rate of profit in relationship to changes in the organic composition of capital overall or to that of American capital specifically. The available statistical surveys do not relate to the marxian categories, but to highly unreliable calculations that emerge from complex market-place occurrences.

These figures do not directly compare the actual profit rate with the actual organic composition of capital. As is the case with individual capitals that can earn extra profits or suffer losses independently of their organic composition, so too the profits that flow to or from a nation's capital are not necessarily tied to its organic composition, but can be co-determined by world market relationships. Because total capital on a global scale, as well as the corresponding organic compositions and rates of surplus-value, are of an unknown size, the rate of profit within a specific country also remains statistically unknown. Bourgeois economics, because of its dependence on statistical measures, focusses not on production, but on the market. Data from this source is only in the narrowest of senses analogous to developments within the production process, from where the marxist categories are derived. Changes in the organic composition of capital, nevertheless, are observable without statistical verification.

The accompanying fall in the profit rate results from the accumulation process itself, without being able to say anything about the actual profitability of capital.

Marx discusses a tendential fall in the rate of profit as part-and-parcel of a rising organic composition of capital. This can be counteracted by a rise in the rate of surplus-value, such that the falling profit rate remains unnoticed. For him, the fall in the profit rate and an accelerated accumulation were one-and-the-same process, an expression of the developing productivity of labour. The profit rate declines because less labour is used in relationship to the existing capital. Less labour and therefore less surplus-labour, or surplus-value, reduces the profit rate that is calculated on total capital. In order to make this intelligible, Marx assumes an accumulation process with an unrealistic assumption of a constant rate of exploitation. Under such artificial conditions, it becomes immediately clear that the rate of profit will not decline if the rate of surplus-value rises sufficiently in relationship to the accumulation process. The tendency of the rate of profit to decline prompts an accelerated accumulation and only in this manner can it be held in check. A slowdown in the accumulation process transforms a tendency for the rate of profit to fall into an actual fall.

If it is only when the accumulation process slows that the empirical side of the tendency for the rate of profit to fall becomes an actual fall, it doesn't make much sense, then, to intuit movement in the rate of profit from the scanty statistics of the last hundred years. The rate of profit does not fall continuously with the growth in the organic composition of capital or its equivalent, the accumulation of capital. The tendency becomes actual during a crisis, when there is a shortage of surplus-value in relationship to that which is necessary for accumulation to continue with adequate profits. It is the re-establishment of a sufficient profit rate that leads to an overcoming of the crisis and a continuation of the process of capital accumulation.

Gillman assumes that I object 'to a test of abstract laws' in which I reject his 'scientific method'. I consider his procedures insufficient, simply because they do not lead to a real test of the marxian law of the falling rate of profit. Empirical verification does not result from a historical-statistical comparison of profit rates with an ever-changing organic composition of capital, but with the crisis-prone nature of capitalist accumulation. Should the accumulation process lower the rate of profit on an ongoing basis, the process will soon come to a halt. Despite interruptions, capitalism has always been able to overcome the inherent tendency of the rate of profit to fall through an enhanced expansion of capital. This process eventually encounters limits which can be traced to the limited ability to expand the exploitation of labour in relationship to capital. When these limits will be reached is not predictable in advance.

Capitalism cannot escape the compulsion to accumulate. This excludes any real perception into the results of the accumulation process. The urgent need for additional capital leads to over-accumulation, that is, to a situation in which the organic composition of capital produces a profit rate that precludes a further expansion. The expansion of capital in terms of value can no longer be borne by the actual production unless the organic composition of capital is lowered or the mass of surplus-value increased. The reaction of capital to a situation of over-accumulation leads on the one hand to structural changes within total capital, in which part is destroyed. On the other hand, it leads to measures that increase the productivity of labour and thereby the mass of surplus-value as well, until a new profit rate allows a new period of expansion. This process occurs as an automatic reaction to crisis conditions, because the determinate processes in the sphere of production are only indirectly intelligible within the market-place.

That the profitability of capital is indirectly lost and then re-established by means of the market, also cannot be explained by market occurrences. These must be explained by reference to the sphere of production – as the production of capital and surplus-value, which sets limits by means of the accumulation process. These limits become visible during economic crises and through the concentration and centralisation of capital that all result from the falling rate of profit. This is simply another manifestation of the law of value, namely, the determination of value and surplus-value through the utilised labour power. Empirical proof for the marxian theory of accumulation can be adduced in this manner, rather than in the deficient statistical investigations which at best reveal that capital accumulates sometimes faster and sometimes slower, a matter that ought to be obvious even without statistical verification.

It was not only a lack of appropriate data that prevented Marx from verifying statistically his theorem regarding the falling rate of profit. He was convinced that the process of capital accumulation would bring into the open the contradictions derived from theory. Capitalist reality is more than just the value theory, even though it can only be grasped by means of this theory. A developmental model of capital accumulation derived strictly from the theory of value is not directly identical with the unfolding capitalist reality. It is a means to perceive this reality, to uncover the secret of its specific motion, without mirroring the chaotic market-place activities. The model is concerned with the dynamics that underpin market events and isolates the essential traits of the capitalist production process. There are aspects of reality, for example, that aren't addressed in the model, just as there are solutions to capitalistically-based problems that are not derived from it – all without impacting the usefulness of the model. My objections [to Gillman] mean only that value theory cannot be strictly compared to the world of capital, without having to conclude that abstract laws must remain without verification.

To reject a statistical test of the falling rate of profit does not imply, as Gillman asserts, that I view Marx's value theory as a pure abstraction that needs no proof and that I refuse 'to translate it into real life'. This 'transformation' can be accomplished without Gillman's statistics. But Gillman's jump directly from value theory to market-based data resembles the many attempts to derive price relations from value relations. All these instances rest on a misunderstanding of Marx's law of value, which of course determines the movement of prices and profits, but not in a manner that is visible. According to Marx, the theory of value is necessary in order to ascertain how prices are determined, since these do not explain themselves. Only an analysis on the basis of the law of value and surplus-value demonstrates the tendency for the rate of profit to fall as a consequence of capital accumulation, which otherwise is not directly visible in actual developments. The law of value is not based on prices and profits at any particular point in time, but on the determination of the general level of prices and the average rate of profit as expressions of the ever-changing productivity of labour.

For Marx, not only prices but also values are fetishistic categories, behind which are hidden historically generated classes and relationships of exploitation. These categories alter nothing about production as a labouring process determined by quantities of time. Within a commodity-producing society like capitalism, the labour process and the economy of time take on the character of value and price relationships. Exploitive relationships appear as the production of value and surplus-value, as a division of the social product between labour and capital. The market transforms the value relations of the production process into price relations. These are recognisable in the theoretically abstract conception of all prices as determined by the labour-time value relationships that coincide with changes in the productivity of labour.

In actuality, there are only prices, and modern economics is occupied with neither value- nor labour-time relationships. For the classical theorists, prices were still derived from labour. The value concept and value relations were not strictly tied to production, however, but instead resulted from a production process characterised by private ownership of the means of production and the appearance of labour power as a commodity. The value concept that results from these conditions was simply the capitalist form in which the underlying necessities of social production are expressed.

The necessity to use and divide labour in such proportions as to guarantee social existence and reproduction occurs in the market-place, behind the backs of the producers. Supply and demand determine the character of the production process, such that an unseen mechanism transforms labour-time determined values into prices. An adequate allocation of social labour ensues. What we are dealing with is a particular division of labour that is not based on actual social needs, but on the value requirements of the competing capitals. Consequently, a difference must be made between a socially unavoidable allocation of labour and the particular form that has been established in capitalism; that is, its subordination under the asocial needs of capital, through which the use and division of social labour is represented as the law of value.

The law of value does not regulate social production and distribution, but the life-cycle of capitalist production and distribution. This regulation exists only insofar as it makes possible social reproduction as the accumulation of capital. The market and price relationships that result from the competitive process offer no insight into the structural and reproductive needs of capitalism as a socially productive system. The social character of capitalist production emerges despite the separate interests of each, but also as a result of these separate interests. The concentration and centralisation of capital as well as the crisis cycle result from the actions of each separate capital, as if each had been forced to act according to the unobserved pressures imposed by capitalist society.

This pressure, e.g. the law of value, does not exist, as do prices, as a real entity, but results from the countless attempts to secure the value of each individual capital. One could say that the law of value exists and that it does not exist, since it relates to the abstract comprehension of concrete processes which are manifested in different forms within capitalism. Accumulation and the fate of each individual capital depend on the accumulation of total capital, determined as they are through the social character of production and the capitalistic division of labour. Total capital becomes a reality only through the actions of the individual capitals, not as a reality that exists separate from them to which they each relate.

Because total production is basically the production of additional capital by means of the individual capitals, the value composition as well as the technical aspects of the organic composition of capital undergo alteration during the course of development. This process is expressed by means of changes in production and prices, which coincide with changes in the use and division of labour even though no special meaning is ascribed to these processes. In this manner, value relations as labour-time relations assert themselves as social necessities of capitalist production only by means of actual price relations within the general process of competition.

It is possible to view this process abstractly in terms of values and labour-time relations. This perspective assumes price relations, without assuming a parallel existence. The attempt, consequently, to extract values from prices, is a practical impossibility, since the opaque market reality does not allow a backwards view of value relations, even though the development of the market is determined by these value relations. This situation justifies the value model of capitalist accumulation, even if it does not allow for quantification in Gillman's sense. Such a model leads away from the inverted world of market-place competition into a world of its underlying material conditions, about which capitalism can alter nothing without eliminating itself.

Prices must deviate from values in order to make capitalist production possible. Simultaneously, they can only be explained as a monetary expression of labour-time quantities, even though the identity of price with value is precluded. The value model, in which a hypothetical total capital equals total labour, results in an accumulation process that is accompanied by a falling rate of profit. The developmental processes are thereby made visible and also overpower any modifications or counter-tendencies. These counter-tendencies can hinder the developmental process, but they cannot halt it altogether.

These counter-tendencies remind us that the model is not to be confused with reality, because the counter-tendencies are not part of the model. The falling rate of profit does not exert its full influence, therefore, as it does in the model. It makes no sense, then, to judge the model of the falling rate of profit even in terms of trustworthy statistics. These only capture the modified movements of a profit rate based on realised profits, which have been thereby determined differently than the organic composition of capital.

Gillman focuses on one of the counter-tendencies, which in his opinion transforms the falling rate of profit into something that happened only in the past. The cheapening of constant capital made it possible to produce 'more surplus-value with less invested capital'. If that were the case, one could say that the tendency of the rate of profit to fall remains latent because of a favourable organic composition of capital. Except for crisis situations, this has always been the case, without necessarily contradicting Gillman's proof of a falling rate of profit in the past. Gillman questions whether 'the relationship of constant capital to variable capital continuously grows with mechanization', and answers negatively due to the mechanisation of constant capital that accompanies growth in the rate of surplus-value. This is not surprising because the rising productivity of labour influences all areas of the productive process, including the part that relates to constant capital. Gillman, however, does not view this process as a result of capitalist accumulation, but rather as 'technical progress' which alters the organic composition of capital in a manner that contradicts the law of value. The falling rate of profit is suspended through technology. This process for Gillman is part of the transition from competitive to monopoly capital, even though there is no direct connection between this transition and technological progress. Monopolisation results from the competitive process regardless of whether or not this has been accompanied by technical progress.

Only within capitalism can one speak of an organic composition of capital. There is an inseparable connection between value and material production in which the rate of profit is determined by the value relationships. The cheapening of constant capital includes the cheapening of the variable capital, which means a higher rate of surplus-value since a smaller proportion of the social product accrues to labour and a larger part to capital. Through this process, capital accumulation is accelerated and the organic composition increased. The development of technology helps to increase the surplus-value and profit, and wherever this is not the case, technological progress also ceases. The same process whereby the organic composition of capital is altered in such a manner that favours profits, leads to an organic composition of capital that is unfavourable to profits. The rising productivity of labour can create a situation in which the variable capital falls in relationship to the constant capital, but only when the rate of growth of constant capital likewise declines.

In Gillman's presentation, technical progress is capable of transforming a deficit of surplus-value into an excess. Because this occurs through the cheapening of constant capital, the excess surplus-value cannot be realised as an accumulation of capital. And because the surplus-value cannot be ceded to the workers, the only remaining solution is its conversion into unproductive expenditures. With these unproductive expenditures, the rate of profit for the productive capital sinks even further, but not as a result of its organic composition. Surplus-value is drained off by the state and channelled into unproductive expenditures, which represent a perverse form of capitalist consumption. This, for Gillman, marks 'the end of capitalism's historic mission', because it has ceased 'to grow as a system of social production'.

With the end of accumulation comes also the end of capitalist production as a value-enhancing process. For Gillman, this is increasingly the case, so that the marxist theory of capital accumulation no longer relates to today's capitalism. The remaining problem is not the production of surplus-value, but of its realisation, a problem that must be solved politically. Viewed economically, technology has already so altered capitalism that a marxist analysis is no longer applicable. Confirmation of this, per Gillman, can be found in the statistical data, even though in the real world, the crisis orientation of capital, as anticipated in the analysis of value, still prevails.

Works Cited

Böhm-Bawerk, Eugen von 2011, *Karl Marx and the Close of His System: A Criticism*, New York: Prism Key Press.
Cole, G.D.H. 1934, *What Marx Really Meant*, New York: Alfred A. Knopf.
Cleaver, Harry 2017, *Rupturing the Dialectic: The Struggle Against Work, Money, and Financialization*, Chico, CA: AK Press.
Engels, Frederick 1884, 'Preface', in Marx 1981.
Gillman, Joseph M. 1958, *The Falling Rate of Profit: Marx's Law and its Significance to Twentieth-Century Capitalism*, New York: Cameron Associates.
Gillman, Joseph M. 1969, *Das Gesetz des tendenziellen Falls der Profitrate*, Frankfurt: Europäische Verlagsanstalt.
Goldwater, Walter 1964, *Radical Periodicals in America, 1890–1950*, New Haven: Yale University Press.
Grossmann, Henryk 1970 [1929], *Das Akkumulations- und Zusammenbruchsgesetz des kapitalistischen Systems*, Frankfurt: Verlag Neue Kritik.
Grossmann, Henryk 1971, 'Die Goldproduktion im Reproduktionsschema von Marx und Rosa Luxemburg', in *Aufsätze zur Krisentheorie*, Frankfurt: Verlag Neue Kritik.
Grossmann, Henryk 1992 [1929], *The Law of Accumulation and Breakdown of the Capitalist System*, abridged, London: Pluto Press.
Grossmann, Henryk [as Grossman] 2013, 'The Change in the Original Plan for Marx's *Capital* and Its Causes', *Historical Materialism*, 21, no. 3: 138–64.
Grossmann, Henryk [as Grossman] 2016, 'The Value-Price Transformation in Marx and the Problem of Crisis', *Historical Materialism*, 24, no. 1: 105–34.
Grossmann, Henryk [as Grossman] 2017, 'The Evolutionist Revolt Against Classical Economics', in *Capitalism's Contradictions: Studies in Economic Theory Before and After Marx*, Chicago: Haymarket Books.
Harich, Wolfgang 1975, *Kommunismus ohne Wachstum? Babeuf und der 'Club of Rome'. Sechs Interviews mit Freimut Duve und Briefe an ihn*, Hamburg: Reinbek.
Hilferding, Rudolf 2011, *Böhm-Bawerk's Criticism of Marx*, New York: Prism Key Press.
Lenin, N. 1921, *'Left Wing' Communism: An Infantile Disorder*, Detroit: Marxian Educational Society.
Linnemann, Hans 1979, *MOIRA: Model of International Relations in Agriculture: Report of the Project Group 'Food for a Doubling World Population'*, Elsevier.
Lukács, Georg 1971, *History and Class Consciousness: Studies in Marxist Dialectics*, Cambridge, MA: The MIT Press.
Luxemburg, Rosa 2015 [1921], *The Accumulation of Capital, or, What the Epigones Have Made Out of Marx's Theory – An Anti-Critique*, in *The Complete Works of Rosa Luxemburg*, Volume 2: Economic Writings 2, London: Verso.

Marx, Karl 1905a, *Theorien uber den Mehrwert*, Volume I, Stuttgart: J.H.W. Dietz.
Marx, Karl 1905b, *Theorien uber den Mehrwert*, Volume II, Stuttgart: J.H.W. Dietz.
Marx, Karl 1909, *Capital*, Volume III, Chicago, Charles H. Kerr & Company.
Marx, Karl 1973a, *Grundrisse: Introduction to the Critique of Political Economy*, New York: Vintage Books.
Marx, Karl 1973b, *Letters to Dr. Kugelmann*, New York: International Publishers.
Marx, Karl 1981 [1884], *Capital*, Volume 2, New York: Vintage Books.
Marx, Karl 1990 [1873], 'Postface to the Second Edition', in *Capital*, Volume 1, London: Penguin.
Mattick, Paul 1969, *Marx and Keynes: The Limits of the Mixed Economy*, Boston: Porter Sargent.
Meadows, Donella et al. 1972, *The Limits to Growth*, New York: Universe Books.
Mesarovic, Maihajlo, and Eduard Pestel 1974, *Mankind at the Turning Point*, New York: Dutton.
Morf, Otto 1951, *Das Verhältnis von Wirtschaftstheorie und Wirtschaftsgeschichte bei Karl Marx*, Bern: A. Francke A.G. Verlag.
Rosdolsky, Roman 1977, *The Making of Marx's 'Capital'*, London: Pluto Press.
Roth, Gary 2013, 'Wild Socialism: All Power to the Councils! A Review of: Martin Comack, *Wild Socialism: Workers Councils in Revolutionary Berlin, 1918–1921*, and Gabriel Kuhn, editor, *All Power to the Councils! A Documentary History of the German Revolution of 1918–1919*', *Insurgent Notes*, December. URL: http://insurgentnotes.com/2013/12/review-wild-socialism-all-power-to-the-councils/.
Roth, Gary 2015, *Marxism in a Lost Century: A Biography of Paul Mattick*, Leiden/Chicago: Brill/Haymarket.
Speier, Hans 1934, 'The Salaried Employee in Modern Society', *Social Research*, February.

Translations and Sources

Translations

'Interview with Paul Mattick (1972)', questions by Peter van Spall, translated by Felix Kurz.
'Capitalism and Ecology', translated by Paul Mattick Jr.
'Henryk Grossman and Crisis Theory', titled and translated by Gary Roth.
'Marxism and Its Critics', titled and translated by Gary Roth.

Thanks to Anne Lopes for her assistance with the translations and to Beliz Yüksel, Danny Hayward, Simon Mussell, and Marlou Meems for their expertise.

Sources

'Obsessions of Berlin': *Partisan Review*, October 1948: 1108–24.
'Authority and Democracy in the United States': *Root and Branch*, no. 7, 1979: 10–14, 27–8.
'Interview with Paul Mattick (1972)': an edited version first appeared as 'Eine Sache namens Sozialismus – Welche Chance hat die Linke? Peter van Spall fragte P. Mattick und R. Schwendter', in *Pardon: Satirische Monatsschrift*, 11, no. 8, August 1972: 30–2.
'Fascism and the Middle Class': *Proletarian Outlook*, 5, no. 3, May–June 1939: 1–5 (grammatical corrections by Gary Roth).
'Capitalism and Ecology': 'Kapitalismus und Ökologie: Vom Untergang des Kapitals zum Untergang der Welt', in Claudio Pozzoli, Herausgebe, *Jahrbuch Arbeiterbewegung*, Band 4, Frankfurt am Main: Fischer Taschenbuch Verlag, 1976: 220–41.
'New Essays': originally published as 'Introduction' to *New Essays*, Westport, CT: Greenwood Reprint Corporation, 1970 (grammatical corrections and title by Gary Roth).
'Dynamics of the Mixed Economy': *Science & Society*, 28, no. 3, Summer 1964: 286–304.
'Henryk Grossman and Crisis Theory': 'Nachwort' in Henryk Grossmann, *Marx, die klassische Nationalökonomie und das Problem der Dynamik*, Frankfurt am Main: Europäische Verlagsanstalt, 1969: 115–33.
'Value Theory and Capital Accumulation': *Science & Society*, 23, no. 1, Winter 1959: 27–51.
'Marxism and Its Critics': 'Nachtrag' in Paul Mattick, *Kritik der Neomarxisten und andere Aufsätze*, Frankfurt am Main: Fischer Taschenbuch Verlag, 1974: 96–105.

Index

abolition of capitalism and social classes 9, 30, 43, 52–53, 68
abstract laws and abstraction 93, 95–99, 108–110, 112–113, 118, 127–131
Africa 67
agriculture 46, 52, 67–68, 74
Aleppo, Syria, 1
alienation 46–47
American capitalism 26–28, 31–38, 41, 85, 114–115, 117, 127
American labour 27–28, 38
America, United States of 1–2, 5, 19–42, 44–45, 65, 68, 70, 72–73, 76, 88–89, 123
anarchism and anarchists 4, 31
anti-capitalism 4, 27
anti-fascism and anti-fascist 31, 74
armaments 7, 50, 64, 81, 83, 86, 125
Asia 3, 33, 40n1, 67, 73
austerity 19, 37
Australia 68
authoritarianism 2, 21, 28–32, 34–37, 40–41, 43, 58, 71

Babeuf, François-Noël 54–55, 58–59
Bauer Otto 94, 99
Berlin 1, 3, 10–25
    See also Germany
Biolat, G. 52
birth control 68
black market 15, 19–24
Böhm-Bawerk, Eugen von 97
bolshevism, Bolsheviks, Bolshevik Party 2–3, 5–6, 18, 31, 48, 50, 55n6, 70n, 71–72, 74–76
bourgeois and bourgeoisie 2, 8, 19, 27–28, 30, 35, 41, 43–44, 46–50, 53, 56, 58, 60, 85, 101–103, 106–107, 117
    bourgeois democracy 27, 29, 71, 92
Brazil 37
breakdown, economic and societal 3, 63, 92, 94, 99–100, 111, 117

capital 7, 9, 27–30, 33–39, 41–44, 46, 48–50, 52, 54, 56, 58–60, 62, 65–68, 74, 78–100, 102–133
    accumulation 7, 27–28, 35, 38, 41, 44, 46–48, 50, 56, 60, 62, 65–66, 80–86, 89, 91–101, 104–114, 116–126, 128–133
    constant and variable 96, 100, 107–108, 112–113, 115, 117, 121, 123, 127, 132–133
    destruction of 86, 89, 105, 121, 124–125
    expropriation of 35, 50, 85
    finance and money 46, 115–116
    foreign 35–36, 49
    industrial 46
    overproduction and over-accumulation 85–86, 110, 118–120, 123, 129
    saving 62, 115, 123
    total and total social 35, 83, 90, 93, 95–97, 99–100, 107–108, 110, 112–114, 118, 120–121, 127–129, 131–132
capitalism, *laissez-faire* 78, 85, 106, 116, 126
    late and post- 8, 34, 42
    monopoly 41, 44, 112, 115, 117, 126, 133
capitalist development 4, 6, 27, 41–42, 44, 47, 49–50, 52, 54, 92, 98, 106, 110, 127
capitalists 11, 29, 36, 41, 44, 46–47, 50, 66, 79, 84–85, 87, 90, 93, 98, 107–108, 116, 119, 122, 126
Carnot, Sadi 51
Central Intelligence Agency (CIA) 37
Chile 37
civil liberties, civil rights, and human rights 26, 30, 35
classless society 34, 43
class society 31, 48, 58
class struggle 26–28, 47–48, 59, 70–71, 100–102
Clausius, Rudolf 51
Club of Rome 3, 51, 53–57, 59–68
colonialism and neo-colonialism 35, 67
commodities 8, 22, 31, 67, 81, 85, 93, 95–96, 100, 103, 106–107, 115–116, 118–121, 130
    glut of 116, 118–119, 121
    overproduction of 8, 85, 100, 118–119, 121
commodity fetishism 43
communism 51–52, 54–60, 68–69, 71–72, 75
Communist International 72
Communist Party 10–11, 15–16, 70–70n

competition   6, 17, 31, 93
  economic   6, 28, 36, 38, 41, 49, 58, 62, 68, 82, 86–87, 90, 98, 106, 109–110, 112, 121–122, 131–132
  political   29, 40
concentration camps, Americans of Japanese extraction   26
  Belsen and Buchenwald   17
  Russian   18
concentration and centralisation of capital   28, 41, 44, 46, 48, 86, 89–90, 124, 126, 129, 131
  of economic and political power   48–50
consumption   5, 56–57, 65, 76–77, 79, 81–84, 89, 94, 104, 117, 119, 123–126, 133
  of raw materials   51, 53–54, 65, 115
  under-consumption   123
  unproductive and non-productive   116, 123, 125
control and ownership of means of production   9, 44, 46–47, 57–58, 78, 102, 126, 130
Coolidge, Calvin   29
council communism   1–2, 70–70n, 72–75
councils   1–2, 5, 51n2, 70–73, 75
  of the unemployed   72
  See also worker's councils, unemployment and unemployed
counter-tendencies   99–100, 104, 111–114, 117, 128, 132
credit   37, 79–80, 98, 105, 109
crisis and crises   1–2, 4–7, 9, 17, 26–27, 73, 100
  ecological   3, 54–57, 59–60, 62–65, 69
  economic   2, 4, 6, 10, 20, 26–28, 34, 36–39, 43, 56, 59, 69–70, 72–74, 76–77, 80, 85–88, 91–94, 99–100, 104–105, 108–112, 116–125, 128–129, 131–133
  theory of   7, 7n, 122

debt   37, 78–80, 85, 88
deficit financing   50, 77, 79–80, 83, 85, 88–89
democracy   2, 4–5, 17, 20–21, 26–38, 40, 43, 49, 59, 71, 92
Democratic Republic of Germany (East Germany or DDR)   51–52, 54, 59
Denmark   9
depreciation   62

depressions, economic See crisis and crises, economic
dialectics, dialectical materialism, dialectical methodology   52–53, 55, 64, 98–99, 111, 117
dictatorship and dictators   1, 18, 21, 26, 35–37, 40–41, 49, 56, 59–60, 71
distribution of commodities   5, 22, 55–56, 58–59, 70, 74, 107, 112, 126, 131
  See also income and income distribution
Dominican Republic   37
Duve, Freimut   52, 56, 58

East (Eastern Europe and Asia)   1, 3, 10, 14, 19, 40–41, 52, 58–59, 61, 69, 89
ecology and ecological   3, 52–66, 68–69
economic policy   46, 50, 65
economic and political power   29, 33, 37, 40–41, 47–49, 66, 70, 73, 86, 102
economics   7–8, 40, 89, 93, 101, 103, 127, 130
  classical   52, 101–103
  marginal utility   103
  subjective value   103
  See also Keynesianism
elections and elected representatives   4, 16, 28–29, 36, 72
Engels, Friedrich   8, 47, 52, 54
England See Great Britain
entropy   51–55
equilibrium   57, 94, 103–104, 106–107, 122–123
  ecological   60–61
Europe   3, 7, 9, 19, 27, 29–31, 41, 72–73, 75, 88–89, 114
exchange-value See value, exchange
expansion of capital and production   7, 33–34, 46, 60, 62, 65, 67–68, 76, 79–92, 94, 105, 109–112, 117–120, 122, 124–126, 128–129
exploitation   20, 27, 29, 32, 35, 41, 44, 48–49, 51, 58–59, 63, 66, 74, 84, 90, 96–97, 110, 112–113, 120, 126, 128, 130
  environmental,   42, 46, 51, 61, 63, 66
  rate, intensity, and limits of   108, 112, 120–122, 128
exports and imports, exporting and exporting   35–37, 67
expropriation   11, 14, 35, 48, 50, 85

fascism and fascists   1–2, 7, 11, 26, 31, 40–42, 48–50, 59, 73
    anti-fascism and anti-fascist   11, 21, 31, 74
forced sterilisation   68
foreign policy   40
France   18, 71, 102
Fulbright, J. William   40

Gaza City, Palestine   1
General Motors   28
German Revolution   3–5, 71, 73
Germany and Germans   3–5, 9, 11–20, 41, 51, 66, 70–73
    See also Berlin
Gillman, Joseph M.   8, 111–118, 122–125, 127–130, 132–133
government-induced production   76–78, 81, 83–85, 87–88, 90–91
Great Britain (England)   19, 71, 88, 102
Great Depression   26, 28, 34, 38, 72, 92, 104
Grossman, Henryk   1, 7, 92–101, 103, 105
growth, economic   6, 34, 51–52, 54–55, 57–61, 63–64, 68, 77–80, 88, 90, 107, 125
    of labour organisations   26–27, 70, 72
    of population   3, 51, 56, 61, 67–68
Grozny (Chechnya)   1
Guatemala   37

Harich, Wolfgang   51–60, 63–66, 68
Harper, J. *See* Pannekoek, Anton
Hegel, Georg W.F.   98
Hibbs, Douglas A.   38
Hitler, Adolf   10, 22, 24, 26
Hungary   71, 75
hunger *See* starvation

ideology   14, 16, 26, 29–30, 34, 38, 47–52, 58, 74, 76–77, 92, 103, 111
imperialism   26, 32–33, 36, 38–39, 41, 43, 49, 73, 75, 86, 93, 114
income and income distribution   38, 46, 63, 76–79, 81–83, 85, 88–90, 121
    national   78, 83, 88–90
India   19, 68
inequality   23, 59, 82
inflation   38, 65, 77, 80–81, 83, 89
internationalism   4

International Council Correspondence   70, 72–73, 75
    See also Living Marxism and *New Essays*
International Monetary Fund (IMF)   37
Internationals, Second, Third, and Fourth   70, 72
investment   35–36, 38, 50, 76–79, 83–84, 88–90, 104, 107, 115, 119–120, 124
    foreign   36
Iran   66
Iron Curtain   17
Italy   9, 41, 71

Jevons, W.S.   103

Keynes, John M.   76–81, 104, 125
Keynesianism   6, 76–77, 80, 85, 125
    liquidity preference   79, 125
    radical   76, 85
Korsch, Karl   1, 73
Krupp Steel Works   66

labour   3, 20, 27–28, 34–35, 41, 44, 46–47, 50, 52, 56, 60, 62–63, 72, 78, 82, 84–86, 89–90, 93, 95–96, 100–103, 106–108, 110, 115–116, 119–122, 128–133
    foreign   36
    movements   2–5, 26–27, 30, 42, 45, 55–57, 60, 70–75, 92, 101
    power   41, 46, 62, 96, 103, 107, 119, 129–130
    -saving   115
    theory of value   8, 92, 95–96, 98, 101–103, 106–107, 111, 129–130
    -time   62, 98, 106, 114, 130–132
    unpaid   41, 119
    white-collar   47
labouring population   64, 107, 125
labour productivity *See* productivity of labour
laissez-faire   76, 78, 85, 106, 116, 126
laws of motion   53, 96
left and left-wing   1–3, 5–7, 9, 39, 42, 44–45, 57, 71–72
leninism and marxism-leninism   53, 58–59, 70*n*
Lenin, Vladimir   52, 72, 98
liberals and liberalism,   7, 30, 33, 40, 42
Linnemann, H.   67

INDEX 141

living conditions and standards 4, 23, 27–28, 37–38, 47, 50, 55–59, 61–62, 66, 68, 84
Living Marxism 72–74
Long, Huey 31
Lukács, Georg 98
Luxemburg, Rosa 1, 4, 7, 9, 75, 92–95, 97, 99, 109

Malthus, Thomas Robert 52, 54–55
Marawi, Philippines 1
Mariupol, Ukraine 1
market, markets, market mechanism, market system 7, 31, 34, 62, 66, 76, 78–91, 93, 96–97, 99–100, 103–104, 106–107, 109–110, 112, 115–116, 118–119, 121–122, 127, 129–132
  black 15, 19–20, 22–24
  capital 37
  labour 27, 120
  stock 121
  Yogoslav socialism 75
  world 20, 34–35, 44, 86, 89, 114, 127
Markgraf, Paul 15
Marshall Plan 15
martial law 37
Marx and Keynes: The Limits of the Mixed Economy 6
Marx, Karl, and marxism 1, 3–4, 6–9, 46–48, 52–55, 58–59, 65, 70, 73–74, 92–120, 122–125, 127–130, 133
  Capital 6, 94, 101
  other works by 95
Massachusetts Institute of Technology (MIT) 38
McCarthyism 32
means of consumption 94
means of production 9, 44, 46–47, 57–58, 62, 78, 94, 102, 107, 120–121, 126, 130
mercantilism 76
Mesarovic, M. 63
middle class 2, 30, 38, 46–49
military 4, 11–12, 17, 33, 35, 37, 41–42, 74, 86–88
minimum wage legislation 82
mixed or dual economy 2, 7, 44, 76–80, 82–85, 88–91, 125
mode of production 42, 52, 62, 65–66, 84, 94, 96, 109, 119, 121

money and monetary matters 20, 29, 36, 72, 76–77, 79–81, 93, 102, 115–116, 121, 132
  taxes and taxation 28, 30, 77–79, 88–90
monopoly and monopolisation 31, 44, 46, 62, 66, 82, 112, 133
  capitalism 30, 41, 44, 112, 115, 117, 122, 126, 133

nationalisation 36, 74
nationalism 21, 75
national liberation 44
Nazism and Nazis (German National-Socialism) 10–11, 13, 15–21, 24, 73
New Deal 26, 27
New Essays 70, 73
New York Times 29, 38
Nixon, Richard 33, 40
  Watergate affair 33

oil 38, 65–66
one-dimensional man 34
organic composition of capital 94–96, 99, 107–108, 113–115, 117, 120, 127–129, 131–133
over-accumulation 86, 110, 119, 129
overpopulation 52, 54, 56, 62, 65–66, 68, 112–113
overproduction 8, 62, 67, 85, 100, 118–121, 123

pacifists 33
Pannekoek, Anton 1, 73
parliamentary systems 36, 40–41, 71–72
  See also elections and elected representatives
party-state 15, 17, 71
patriotism 34
People's Front 49
Peru 37
Pestel, E. 63
Pieck, Wilhelm 11, 15
Poland 75
polarisation 46, 49–50
police 2, 5, 15, 17, 22, 32, 34, 42, 102
political economy 98, 102, 107, 111
political institutions 26, 35, 42
political power 29, 33, 40–41, 48–49, 70, 86, 102
politics and the political 1–6, 8–10, 17–18,

22, 26–41, 43, 47–48, 52, 56, 61, 64–65, 70–75, 86–87, 89, 101–102, 125–126, 133
politicians   16, 21, 32, 34, 40, 42
poverty and the poor   5, 18–19, 42, 56, 68, 81–82, 123
prices   8, 20, 22, 37, 61, 65–66, 80, 82, 90, 94, 96–98, 102–104, 106–107, 113, 121–122, 130–132
private production   78–79, 87–88
private property   29, 35, 89, 121
private sector   2, 78, 83, 90, 125
production, conditions of   44, 110, 120
  foreign   36
  government-induced   76–78, 81, 83–85, 87–88, 90–91
  national   79–81
  relations of   27, 44, 54, 56, 58, 61, 93, 102–107, 119
  social   80, 83–84, 88, 91, 107, 124, 126, 130–131, 133
  See also means of production, mode of production, overproduction, waste production
productive forces   47, 49, 52, 54–55, 58, 61–62, 65, 100, 106–107, 109–110, 123
productive labour   62, 116
productive power   54, 60, 62, 100
productivity   67–68, 80, 83, 85, 106–107, 118, 122
productivity of labour   28, 50, 52, 60, 82, 84, 90, 95, 100, 106–108, 115–116, 121, 128–130, 132–133
profit and profitability   3, 8, 15, 20, 28, 35, 37, 41–42, 47–48, 50, 54, 62, 65–66, 77–85, 87, 89–90, 93, 98–100, 102, 104, 107–108, 110–114, 116, 118–122, 124–125, 127–130, 132–133
  rate of   8, 65, 81, 83, 90, 96, 99, 113, 115, 119–120, 122, 127–130, 133
  falling rate of   65, 94–96, 99–100, 104, 108–109, 111–120, 122–124, 127–130, 132–133
  total   66, 83
  See also counter-tendencies
proletarian and proletariat   44, 46–50, 56–60, 70–71, 101, 126
  See also labour, working class
Proletarian Party   70n, 72
propaganda   10, 15–17, 20–21, 24, 70

property   35, 43, 47, 50, 52, 56, 58, 62, 67, 90, 121
  See also private property
prosperity   4, 6, 36, 57, 76–77, 83, 89–90, 100, 105, 111, 123
public opinion   31, 34
public sector   78, 83, 88, 125
public works   50, 77, 81, 83, 87

racial minorities   32, 34, 45
radicalism and radicals   1–7, 9, 32, 42, 45, 48, 72, 76, 92
raw materials   54, 56–57, 59, 61–65, 67, 115
realisation of profits and surplus-value   8, 84, 93, 100, 112–116, 118–119, 122–125, 133
recessions *See* crisis and crises, economic
redistribution of income   82–83, 90
Red Scare   32
reformism   30, 75, 92, 101
reforms, economic and social   4, 20, 41–42, 47–48, 52, 91–92
repression   32, 34, 37, 42, 57
reproduction   41, 58, 78, 94, 107, 126, 130–131
  simple and expanded   56, 94–97, 99, 107, 120
revisionism   8, 57–58, 92
revolution   5–6, 8, 39, 43–44, 49–50, 54, 56–57, 59–61, 68, 70–76, 92, 101, 115
Ricardo, David   52, 55, 102
Roosevelt, Franklin   26, 40
Rosdolsky, Roman   98–99
Rühle, Otto   73
rugged individualism   38
ruling or capitalist class   27–29, 31, 40, 42, 44, 46–48, 59–61, 93, 126
Russian Revolution   32, 55n, 70, 74
Russia (Soviet Union) and Russians   1, 3–5, 7, 10–18, 20, 40n, 49, 54, 61, 67, 71, 74

Sanaa, Yemen   1
science   19, 43, 53, 57, 60–61, 103
Siemens   3, 5
social democracy and social democrats   4, 70n, 74, 92
Social Democratic Party of Germany   3–6, 71, 74
socialism and socialists   2–5, 9, 27, 29, 31, 33, 42–45, 48–50, 55–60, 64, 70–71, 73–76, 92, 101–102, 111

INDEX 143

social policy   92
social revolution *See* revolution
social system   2, 6, 31, 62, 102
Socialist Unity Party (East Germany)   15, 16
South America   35, 67
soviets   70–71
　See also workers' councils
Spain   74
stagnation   7, 47–49, 76, 78, 81, 84, 91, 116–118, 124
Stalin, Joseph, and stalinism,   51, 58
starvation   15, 17, 20, 22–25, 50, 56, 67
state capitalism or state-run system   3, 7, 35, 40–41, 43–44, 49, 58, 60–62, 74, 91, 125–126
state power   41, 58–59
surplus-labour   100, 107–108, 114, 128
surplus product   56, 58, 61, 81, 107
surplus-value   8, 47, 56, 61, 64–66, 93, 96, 98–101, 103–110, 112–130, 132–133
　mass of   8, 66, 108, 116, 118, 120–121, 123, 129
syndicalism and syndicalists   4, 27, 31, 74

technology and technocrats,   34, 40–41, 43, 54, 60–61, 105, 115–117, 123–124, 132–133
terror and terrorism   10, 13–16, 18, 21, 23, 26, 32, 37, 87
thermodynamics   3, 51, 53
Third World   35, 55
Titania Palast   19
totalitarianism   19, 26, 31–35, 37, 61
Tovarisch   11
trade, foreign and international   35–36, 98, 112–114
two-party system   27

Ulbricht, Walter   51
unemployment and unemployed   5, 38, 56, 72–73, 76–77, 81, 88, 104–105, 116, 120–121, 125
unions and trade unions   3–5, 16, 27–28, 45, 71–72
United Workers Party   72
USSR *See* Russia

value   8, 89, 93–94, 97–103, 106–113, 120–122, 124, 129–133

　exchange-   95, 97, 99, 103–104, 107, 109, 121
　law of/theory of/abstract analysis of   8, 93, 95–99, 101–103, 106–113, 118, 127–133
　use-   62, 94–95, 103, 110, 121
　See also surplus-value
Vietnam and Indochina Wars,   32, 41–42, 44–45
violence   30, 68, 124
Volkssturm   11
Volkswagen Foundation   61

wage and wages   4, 15, 27–28, 30, 33, 38, 46, 82–83, 85, 102, 107, 112–113, 122
wage-labour   44, 93, 96
wage struggles   28, 31, 47
war   3–4, 6, 12, 14, 17–19, 21–23, 26, 33–34, 39, 42, 45, 48–50, 55, 64–66, 69–70, 73–74, 76, 78–80, 84, 86–89, 92, 105, 111, 124–125
　anti-   4, 21, 33
　atomic   43, 64–65, 69, 87
　civil   42, 50, 74
　post/post-World War II/cold   1, 6, 20, 32, 34, 87
　economy   79–80, 84, 88
　socialism   76
　World War I   3–4, 6, 26, 31–32, 48, 64, 76, 80, 92, 111, 115
　World War II   1, 6, 40, 64, 72–75, 77, 80, 87, 89, 105
　See also Vietnam and Indochina Wars
waste production   7, 62, 64, 81, 83–84, 86–89, 91, 116, 123, 125
wealth   42, 47, 49–51, 54–55, 58, 66, 78, 104
welfare   30, 38, 77, 82, 87, 125
West   1, 13–14, 17–18, 20–21, 40–41, 49, 52, 58–59, 61, 66, 69, 71, 75, 88
Western Europe   9, 70*n*, 72, 75, 88–89
workers' councils   1–2, 5, 43, 51*n*, 70–75
workers' movement *See* socialism and socialists
working class and workers   2–6, 9, 26–28, 30, 32–33, 38–39, 41, 43–50, 56–61, 63, 66, 69–74, 90, 92–93, 98, 100, 102, 107, 113, 122, 126, 133
　See also proletariat; labour

Yugoslavian market socialism   75

www.ingramcontent.com/pod-product-compliance
Lightning Source LLC
Chambersburg PA
CBHW070632030426
42337CB00020B/3990